HISTORY AND KASHMIR POLITICS (1947-2017)

HISTORY AND KASHMIR POLITICS (1947-2017)

By

Dr. Raj Kumar

Miss Ramiyan Bhardwaj

KALPAZ

First Published, 2018

Published by

Kalpaz Publications
C-30, Satyawati Nagar,
Delhi – 110052
Ph.: 011-47034999, 9811692060
www.kalpazpublications.com
E-mail: kalpaz@hotmail.com

Printed at: G. Print Process, Delhi

Cataloging in Publication Data—DK
Courtesy: D.K. Agencies (P) Ltd. <docinfo@dkagencies.com>

Kumar, Raj, Dr., author.
History and Kashmir politics (1947-2017) / by Dr. Raj Kumar, Miss Ramiyan Bhardwaj.
pages cm
ISBN 9789386397799 (HB)

1. Jammu and Kashmir (India)—Politics and government. 2. Jammu and Kashmir (India)—History. I. Bhardwaj, Ramiyan, author. II. Title.

LCC DS485.K27R57 2018 | DDC 954.6 23

Contents

Acknowledgement

In course of drafting this book entitled *"History and Kashmir Politics"*, author was inspired by my co-writer Miss Ramiyan Bhardwaj (daughter), student of *"Mass Communication and New Media"* known as a Dalit Agency of the Dogra State. The topic of this draft is partly based on the burning history of "*Kashmir Issue*" called 'Religion' and the peace settlement with India and Pakistan. Thus, the conservative society of Kashmir diverted from the basic issues called "Spirituality" and converted into "*Brahminmat*" due to dirty politics of the Islamabad and Islamic view of the advance society-Radha Soami culture.

I am thankful my brothers and sisters, daughters and son, they provided me enough wit to write down on this topic; I am also thankful Prof. Perminder Kour who provided me valuable suggestions on this topic.

My especial thanks are due for the Kalpaz Publication Direct, Mr. Amit Garg and the staff members-Delhi.

Foreword

Brian Hines writes, "The soul then takes great pleasure in hearing what has been called" "Kashmir Issue" politics of Negativism. He continues with the following observations: "Holy Spirit" or Nam-History. Moreover, Richard Rolle described in his study pertaining to "Kashmir Issue" and its politics Young India or the message of world peace and the development of history as a dialogue between the *haves* and *have-nots* = Karl Marx ka Vichar "Haves" are eating more and crying more, whereas, "have-nots", who are eating less, and work in silence, having "Reality" base knowledge and a critique of spiritual fascism.

Dr. Shabnam Grewal

Preface

The authors of this book have noted the event of '*Kashmir Issue*' after the death of Burhan Wani, Militant issue, Sixteen thousands crores of property of Kashmir was damaged, on Islamic Religions Aggression, 'Blind Faith Ke Theory'. Many Semi-mythical character have been emerged in the Kashmir State, Dalit Issue, Morgan Ke Classical Society, no reality. '*Rites and rituals*' like Roza and Navarathra, Pahari customs and ceremonies, rules and conventions were held in the Masjid, proved failure there is no substance of the Reality propaganda of the spirituality, Manmat Ke Story, there is no will of God, prevailed in the Muslim society. Saints of all the ages, ancient to modern man, they left the message of God and brotherhood of man. Where stands the message of NC, PDP, Congress, Group discussion. Moreover, they have no objective in their lifestyle, political mongers, money grabbers, and befooling the Dalits or the minority community of the Jammu region. They are more advance as that of Pt. Kalhana of Kashmir and followed by M.A. Stein, a great scholar of the Dalit Christianity, true historian.

Miss Ramiyan Bhardwaj

Introduction

This book entitled "*History and Politics of Kashmir*" = Dalit history of a great Sudra of Jammu and his family = Holy Quranic Ideology.

"*History is the product of two great forces, God and Man*"; the course of action which were seen in Kashmir valley after Burhan Wani = Blind Faith Ke Theory. According to the Sufi Saints scholar of India from the very beginning of the man, our actions are so important instead of the Religious propaganda = bigotry race of North India (Kashmir); that in which the manners reflected through agitation and controlled by the "law" as pressure building technique to leave Kashmir as Independent State. Only Sunni Muslims, they were favour in that, as the local politics of Kashmir, but they could not quit from India. In the book '*The Path of the Masters* (pp. 1-7), Dr. Julian Johnson writer, "at length on the implications of the law of action" = Dr. B.R. Ambedkar Ke Soch and "reaction for death and for life" = Naya Kashmir.

"*Human Rights*" belong to everyone, yet horrific violations seen in the Kashmir Valley after the death of Burhan Wani Manmat Ka Kathama New history of the Jammu and Kashmir State there is a movement of *Civic Institution*s called RUSA, RAMSA, etc.

Over the past two decade, there was a militancy in Kashmir, before it, it was in Punjab wherestands the ideology of *'Human Rights'* of both the male and female Dalits and anti Dalits. Anti-Dalits have no history 'rites and ritual' Ke Soch Brahminism either, he or she is Hindu and Muslims; third force Dalits. Dalits, they need food, clothing and shelters; they are history creators, whereas history of other groups of India like Ambani, Birla, Tata etc. They dominated the society with money power and muscle power by providing fund to the Govt. agencies big politicians of India for the functioning of State and to suppress the Dalits.

Women play a role in the economics of every country on the planet to fulfill the demand of their childrens equal like male. For example, a madam of the Govt. Gandhi Nagar for women, named Kamlesh Salathia, lecturer in Geography. She is nice lady in her behavior = having no knowledge of the Rajput history = Civilized Lady, but in Muslim Society, there is great hue and cry led by women.

"Human Rights" refer to the basic rights' as Shahjahan provided to his wife Mumtaz Dr. Shabnam Grewal and Raj Rishi of Jammu and Kashmir State. Twenty eight years have been passed to see to each other, but she uses to live in my heart and mind as she is an alive woman of the human technology. "*Kashmir politics*", after, 1947 dominated the entire region of the State majority group of the Muslims and well educated in Quranic lores as Hindus of BJP. Minority group meant for spiritualism Chamar Megh Batwal baradari less politics, less employment. Equality stands in their "*Constitution*" as upper class society. To make up the problem of Dalit community; author did politics with the Lord and wrote number of books on human history Chamar thought tanner view of the Kashmir found in *Rajatarangini*. Kashmir politics is presently in a state of great influx due to their mutual rivalries. Whereas, the Dogri or Pahari speaking area of Jammu region Dalits, they are in a fix as good human beings, dominated by the negativism.

Dalit Christian Science as a Religion

Christian Science is one more of the considerable number of offshoots from orthodox Muslims Blind Faith Ke Theory Rites and Rituals concept. The student of Islam first deal with the Master Zinda Pir, having the status of God. Mind is the Chief instrument of 'spirit' *Early History of Jammu Region* (Pre-historic to 600 A.D) *A Primitive History of Untouchables* unpublished material of the scholar. Mind has its methods of operation Dalit history. '*History of Chamar Dynasty*" (600-1200) Reserve category Ka document and absence period of Indian history. Julian Johnson, again, writes, "In what is called the subconscious reservoir of mind, there lies an almost limitless store of energy", about Azadi destructive term in modern nations, Religion stands nowhere in "politics". "Politics" would be positivism Pakistan Ke Government jealous feeling or propaganda of the modern world and Human History.

Spiritualism

This movement can hardly be called a Religious movement in Kashmir as propaganda of this exploited term. The word religion comes from the root 're', meaning 'back' to the ancient period of India, when there were no Masjid, no Mandir Vedic Age, Age of the Aryan. Rites and Rituals, like

Rozas and Navrathra, stand, nowhere in Dalit History Murshid Ka Gian Living Being Deity Ka Ideology. (C.W. Sanders, *The Inner Voice*; pp. 1-47). History Repeat itself recitation view of Holy Quran true value Holy Ghost of the Murshid exploited by Hamim Gujjar of Kashmir converted the modern society non-vegetarians. Vegetarian view is of the Living Master. The young militant Bhurhan Wani = Saheed Bhagat Singh, born after the 1989 upsurge, epitomizes, the new generation and it was the biggest test for the BJP hardline Hindu+Muslims, PDP for the welfare of the state is the builder of the modern India = Dr. B.R. Ambedkar. He is the real founder of the modern state of India. This book "*History and Kashmir Politics*", begins with the period of Prophet Mohammad and Durlabhavaradha-I of Kashmir as a separate state of mind = Pakistan and Indian Union = One thought of the social-history. **Note.** With the recent study of the Walkout Assembly procession, they appeared like monkeys snakes, animals, etc. It appears that they have no knowledge of the *"Good Faith"* (2018) and constructive view of the human technology.

Chapter - 1

The Prophet Muhammad

Part - One

The Period of Ignorance

Towards the beginning of the seventh century CE, the political and cultural landscape of both the Near and Middle East was dominated by two great empires. From its capital Constantinople (now Istanbul), the eastern Roman Empire controlled most of the shoreline of the Mediterranean as well as the lands at its eastern end. Further east lay the Persian Empire, with its capital Ctesiphon in the early decades of the century, these two empires were at war with each other. Under Chosroes II, the Persians embarked on a conquest of the Roman eastern provinces. Their progress was swift: western Mesopotamia, Egypt, Syria, Armenia and part of Anatolia all fell within a few years, during which the Persians took Jerusalem and captured Christendom's most sacred relic, the Holy Cross. In 622 the Romans were strong enough to launch a counter-offensive and by 629 Heraclius-I had reconquered the lands taken by the Persians. He also returned the Holy Cross to Jerusalem, symbolizing the triumph of Christianity over Zoroastrianism, a religious tradition already in decline. Heraclius then overhauled the civil and military administration of the Empire, and Greek rather than Roman was adopted as the official language. In recognition of these cultural changes, historians refer to the old eastern Roman Empire, from the reign of Heraclius onwards, as the Byzantine Empire, Byzantion having been the Greek name for Constantinople before Constantine made it his capital = Property Statement.

On the southern edge of these mighty empires lay a very different culture that of the nomadic Arabic-speaking Bedouin tribes of the Arabian Peninsula.

Each tribe was autonomous, but a number of shared values were common to them all: loyalty to the family, clan, or tribe; pride in the ancestral lineage; and a love of independence. Tribal leadership was sometimes inherited directly, but leaders could also be appointed by general consensus when they exhibited the necessary personal qualities. Social stability and cohesion were maintained by the loyalty of the tribes' members and, in return, the tribe's wealth and possessions were shared generously among them. On the bigger scale, the vendetta-like code of justice which operated between the tribes prevented any one tribe from obtaining dominance over the others. At the same time, the constant warfare between the tribes made it impossible for the Arab people to unite behind a common purpose and found a civilization of their own. This lack of unity was to some extent reflected in their religious beliefs, at present it found in Jammu and Kashmir region.

In contrast to the monotheistic religions of the neighbouring Byzantine and Persian Empires the Arabs had a pantheon of pagan deities. Although they worshipped at the deities' shrines, the focal point of worship for the Arabs was the massive cube-shaped shrine of the *"Kaba"*, which stood at the heart of an ancient sanctuary (*baram*) in Mecca. Known as the Holy House or House of God. it was dedicated to *al-Lab*, the High God of the Arab pantheon. The Kaba was also the setting for an annual pilgrmage *(haj)* lasting several days, tinting which hostilities between warring tribes were suspended as Arabs from all over the peninsula made their way to Mecca to perform the traditional rites and rituals. These included circling around the Ka'ba and touching the Black Stone set in one of its corners.

Before the seventh century had run its course this ancient sanctuary was to become the focal point for the emergent monotheistic Religion of Islam, which, like Judaism and Christianity, traces its origins back to Abraham (Ibrahim). The Qur'an relates that the foundations of the Ka'ba were raised by Abraham and Ishmael (Qur'an 2:125ff,) at the place where, in submission to God's command, Abraham had made ready to sacrifice Ishmael, his son by his bondwoman (slave) Hagar. In the biblical Book of Genesis, Abraham demonstrated his submission to the Will of God by preparing to sacrifice Isaac, his son by his wife Sarah (Genesis 22). Genesis also tells how, prior to the sacrifice of Isaac, Hagar and her son had been abandoned in the desert at Sarah's request. Abraham was displeased at this but God reassured him, saying that, like Isaac, Ishmael would become the father of a nation. The account of Hagar's wandering in the desert is similar in both holy books, and many of the rituals in the annual pilgrimage to Mecca commemorate events that occurred in the haves of Abraham, Hagar and Ishmael. But we have jumped ahead of ourselves by making the connection between Islam and the Ka'ba. It is time to return to Mecca as it was at the end of the pre-Islamic period; a time known to Muslims as *al-jahiliyyab* (the Period of Ignorance).

Mecca

The Early Years

Muhammad was born in Mecca in 570 CE into the Hashim clan of the Quraysh tribe. A few generations earlier, the Quraysh had abandoned their nomadic way of life to become guardians of the sanctuary (Gujjar) and at the time of Muhammad's birth they were the most powerful and prestigious tribe in Mecca. They were also highly successful traders and had turned Mecca into one of the most important cities in Arabia. The trade route linking the Mediterranean with southern Arabia and the Indian Ocean passed close to the city Caravans would make a detour to visit the holy site and the suspension of hostilities that coincided with the pilgrimage enabled the Arabs in Mecca to trade the one another in peace.

Orphaned at an early age - his father, Abdullah, had died before he was born, and his mother, Aminah, before he was six - the young Muhammad was brought up by his grandfather 'Abd al-Mutallib. During the hajj' Abd al-Mutallib provided food and water for the pilgrims. He was also responsible for the upkeep of the Well of Zamzam (from which Hagar had obtained water (during her desert sojourn with Ishmael), and so the young Muhammad would have acquired an intimate knowledge of the religious beliefs of the pagan Arabs. While watching over the family's flocks in the hills around Mecca, he would also have grown accustomed to periods of solitude in the arid landscape of Arabia. When he was eight he went to live with his maternal uncle, Abu Talib, who, like Muhammad's grandfather, was connected with the religious rituals of the Meccan sanctuary. He was also a merchant, and when Muhammad was about twelve years old he began to take him on trading trips, sometimes lasting several months. As the years passed, Muhammad's impeccable conduct in business earned him a reputation for honesty and he became known as the 'Trusted One' (*al-Amin*) Nam or Kalma. While still a young man, he entered the employment of Khadijah, a wealthy widow some fifteen years his senior; and looked after her trading interests. They were married when Muhammad was twenty-five and Khadijah was forty. Of their seven children only their daughter Fatimah survived beyond childhood.

The transition from nomadic poverty to sedentary affluence had not been easy for the Quraysh. Their new position brought with it a decadence in which traditional tribal values were replaced by the unbridled pursuit of worldly wealth. Within the tribe itself, each of the clans or family units fought each other for a share of the riches, a situation that contrasted strongly with the earlier ethos whereby the tribal wealth was shared equally amongst its members. This new state of affairs led to considerable inequalities between rich and poor, whereas previously the wealthier members of the tribe had seen it as their duty to care for the poor. This did not go unnoticed by Muhammad who, as a trader, had acquired a reputation for fair dealing. He saw it leading to the disintegration of both tribal and social structures of the ancient and early medieval history.

'Recite!'

As the years passed, Muhammad = Brain's study took to meditating for long periods in a cave of Mount Hira, outside Mecca. It was there, during a retreat in the month of Ramadan in 610, when he was about forty years old, that he received his first revelation in the form of a dramatic visitation from the Archangel Gabriel (*Jibreel*). It was night and Muhammad was either asleep or in a deep meditative state when the angel came to him and commanded: 'Recite!' (iqura!) in reply. Muhammad protested: 'I am not a reciter.' (A 'reciter' (Kabin) was someone who went into an ecstatic trance and claimed to utter prophetic oracles. Muhammad was protesting that he was not one of these people.) The angel tonic him in a powerful embrace, holding him ever tighter until both his breath and his strength had been squeezes from him. Then the angel released him and commanded: 'Recite!'. Again Muhammad protested: 'I am not a reciter'. The angel took hold of him, embraced him hard a second time, released him when he was on the point of exhaustion and commanded: 'Recite!'. Again he protested: 'I am not a reciter'. For a third time the angel took him in an overpowering embrace and commanded:

> Recit*e: In the name of your Lord who created — created man from* a dot of blood!
>
> Recite: Your Lord is the Most Bountiful One, who by the pen taught man what he did not know! (Qur'an 96: 1—5)

Muhammad, who is described as an ummi an 'unlettered' (that is, illiterate) one, found himself reciting the "Word of Allah". With the descent of the Qur'an (meaning 'Recitation') as 'history repeat itself', Muhammad's mission as Prophet and Messenger had begun. Islamic tradition holds that on that particular night the entire Qur'an descended into the spiritual heart of the Prophet. It was to take many more revelations, given during the remaining twenty-three years of the Prophet's life, for this 'vertical' descent to be transmitted 'horizontally' — that is, for the entire Qur'an to be expressed in physical words. We shall be turning to the Qur'an in greater detail in the next chapter. For now we stay with the night the Qur'an was received, known as the Night of Power *(laylat-a1-qadr)* Dalit History when the angels and spirits descended:

> Lo! We revealed it on the Night of Power (Qadr).
> Ah, what will convey unto thee what the Night of Power is!
> The Night of Power is better than a thousand months.
> On that night the angels and the Spirit descend, by the permission of their Lord, with His decrees.,
> That night is peace, till break of dawn.
> (Qur'an 97:1—5)

The Night of Power was nor Muhammad's first encounter with the Archangel Gabriel. Prior to his mother's death, he had experienced what is known as the '*Splitting Open of the Breast*' (*shaqq as-sadr*) or '*Breast Washing*'. On this occasion Gabriel had seized him and pushed him to the ground. His breast was split open, his heart removed and purified of a dark substance in it. After the purification of the heart, the Archangel replaced it, healed the Prophets breast and went on his way. According to tradition, a similar experience occurred at other times in his life. In his book The Islamic Tradition, Professor Victor Danner explains the esoteric significance of this event:

> Symbolically the event points to the removal of ignorance represented by the dark substance, through the intervention of supernatural purification. The result is an unveiled or purified heart source of impeccant [infallible] conduct thereafter. The celestial agent in the story is Gabriel — or in other accounts angelic beings who blot out the transmitted legacy of the Fall. There is something prototypal in the whole sequence of events: mystical rebirth is implied therein. Muhammad's inward, celestial and chosen mature makes his outward, human nature conform to this primordial purity by removing all obstacles to its radiance. In the process the resulting impeccance (ismah) of the rasul [meaning to 'Messenger'] is a lesson to the believer of mystical bent that he,too, must restore in himself the Edenic image through the

> elimination of the darkened clouds that cover the inner eye of the heart. (Victor Danner, The Islamic Tradition, 41)

In this passage Professor Danner mentions several themes to which we will be returning later; ignorance, a purified heart, the relationship between inner and outer natures and the eye of the heart. The imagery associated with the heart is of particular significance, for the Way of the Sufi is often referred to as the 'Way of the Heart' Sufis also talk of polishing the heart. This is not so that they can see themselves in it more clearly! Rather, polishing the heart signifies the erasure of the image of the individual 'self' which cover's the eye of the to heart like a veil. A polished beast reflects nothing but God. The veiling of the heart is an example of *ghaflah* (forgetfulness). Its opposite is *dhikr* (recollection or remembrance of God), the practice of which is the most effective way to polish the heart.

An essential part of Muhammad's message concerned another type of purification, the purification of the Ka'ba of its pagan idols for Allah commanded: '*Purify My House*' Sudra Family (Qur'an 2:125). With the removal of the idols from the sanctuary; the Ka'ba would return to the purpose for which it was intended: the worship of Allah alone. In other words, polytheism (*shirk*) would give way to monotheism (tawbid). But whereas our Western understanding of polytheism (*poly*, many; *theos*; god) aid monotheism tends to be in the net row sense of many gods aid one God the sense implied by the words *shirk* and *tawbid* is rather different.

To quote Professor Danner again. *Tawbid* ("Divine Unity") "Holy word" is the recognition that the Divinity Allah is the One who has no second no associate no patents no offspring no peers (Danner; *The Islamic Tradition,* 4), *Shirk* the opposite of *tawbid* is to attribute to 'any' being or thing an existence that is outside or independent of the Divine Unity. As Allah asks in the Qur'an, 'Have you seen those who made gods of their own passions?' (25:43). In this regard, the decadent lifestyle and sense of self-sufficiency (*istaqa*) exhibited by the wealthier members of the Quraysh was tantamount to a declaration of independence from Allah's. The early Suwar (singular Surah or Chapter) of the Qur'an are a reminder of Allah's benevolence. As Karen Armstrong, the writer and broadcaster, says:

"The Qur'an was not teaching the Quraysh anything new. Indeed, it constantly claims to be 'a reminder' of things known already, which it throws into more lucid relief. Frequently the Qur'an introduces a topic with a phrase like: 'Have you not seen Allah?' or 'Have you not considered Him?' The Word of God was not issuing arbitrary commands from on high but was entering into dialogue with the Quraysh. It reminds them, for example, that the Ka'ba, the House of al-Lah accounted in large measure for their success which was really in some sense owing to God. The Quraysh loved to make the ritual circumambulations around the shrine but when they put themselves and their own material success at the centre of their Lives they had forgotten the meaning of these ancient rites of orientation. They should look at the 'signs' (ayat) of God's goodness and power in the natural world. If they failed to reproduce God's benevolence in their own society, they would be out of touch with the true nature of things. (Karen Armstrong; A History of God; P 166)

'Orientation' is a key word here, for it means more than simply pointing oneself physically in a particular direction. It also refers to our inner orientation, whether this is towards ourselves — that is, to our ego-personality or towards something much greater, to the source on which we depend for our being = Negative Islam, like Roza tradition, etc. Orientation towards the latter entails an act of submission, the surrender (*Islam*) of our whole being to the Divine Will. (A person who surrenders his or her whole being in this way — that is, practices Islam — is a *Muslim*). Without this total surrender we remain oriented towards our ego- personality, and subject to its every whim and desire. From a certain point of view, however, there is no separation between what we refer to as our 'inner' and 'outer' lives. Our outer life corresponds to our inner state. For this reason the ritual prayers (*salat*) instigated by Muhammad involved the physical act of bowing down, an outer gesture which both confirmed and would help to develop the inner orientation.

Knowing that his message would not go down well with the proud Quraysh. Muhammad refrained from preaching publicly for a period of about three years. Instead he delivered his message in private. Those who accepted his Prophethood in these early years were few. Tradition relates that Khadijah, his loyal and supportive wife, was the first, followed by 'Ali, his cousin. Others began to follow in increasingly large numbers.

When Muhammad's teaching first came to the attention of the Quraysh they did not object, thinking it to be just another money-making cult to add to the many already using the Ka'ba and the sanctuary. All this changed in 613 when Muhammad began preaching publicly. He called upon the Meccans to reject the many different pagan religions, to remove the idols from the Ka'ba and to surrender to Allah, the One and Only God, the God of Abraham and all the Prophets. In so doing he not only challenged the position of power and wealth enjoyed by the Quraysh as guardians of the sanctuary, but he also threatened to undermine part of the traditional way of life of the Arab people.

The response of the Quraysh was predictably hostile. Why should they give up their wealth and prestige? Yet by preaching a return to the religion of Abraham, Muhammad continued to gain the acceptance of his teaching, especially among the smaller clans like "Gargotra" in Jammu and Kashmir State. The situation came to a head in 616, when Muhammad ùsêd his position as one of the guardians of the Ka'ba to deliver his message to the wider audience of pagan tribesmen, who came from all over Arabia to worship in the sanctuary. Some of the elders of Muhammad's clan, the Hashim, now turned against him because of a boycott imposed on their merchants by the other clans of the Quraysh. As hostility increased, some seventy or so of Muhammad's followers fled to Ahyssinia, where they sought the protection of Negus, the Christian ruler.

The Night Journey (Isra) and Ascent (Mi'raj)

One evening Muhammad was by the Ka'ba, 'in a state between sleeping and waking', when Gabriel (*Jibreel*) appeared to him and told him to mount a winged beast called Buraq. The animal, which was 'smaller than a mule and larger than an ass', had a woman's head and a peacock's tail. Muhammad's wondrous steed took him to Jerusalem,' to the site of the ruined Temple of Solomon, where Abraham (*Ibrabim*), Moses (Musa), Jesus (*Isa*) and all the other Prophets were gathered. Muhammad led them in prayer, and then Buraq bore him upward to the Seventh Heaven. As they passed through each of the seven heavens he met one or another of the Prophets who had preached the Oneness of God to humankind as Radha Soami mission of the modern time.

While in Heaven, the Voice of Allah informed Muhammad about the obligatory prayers he and his followers would he required to perform. On his way out he passed Moses, who asked him about the prayers. Muhammad told him that Allah had commanded them to pray fifty times a clay. Moses suggested that this was too heavy a burden arid counselled Muhammad to beg Allah to reduce it. His request was granted and it was established that the obligatory prayers were to be repeated five times a day by sharing 50 minutes each and above in the form Buddha state of mind (a figure that cotticitles with the number of our physical senses = study of Dalit literature). Buraq then carried Muhammad back to Mecca that same night.

The Night Journey from Mecca to Jerusalem (*al-isra'*) and Muhammad's Ascent (*al-mi'raj*), which are described in the Qur'an (*Surah*

17) and many Prophetic traditions, are of key importance in the Islamic tradition they are commemorated in the annual festival of the Night of Ascent (*laylat al-miraj*). The site on the Temple Mount in Jerusalem from which Muhammad ascended to Heaven is marked by the Dome of the Rock, Islam's most holy shrine outside Mecca. (Built c.691, some sixty years after the death of Muhammad, it is one of the first and purest examples of Islamic architecture.) The esoteric teaching associated with the *isra'* and *mi'raj* is explained by Professor Danner:

"The movement horizontally from Mecca to Jerusalem at night has relations with the self-extinction, **'the dark night of the soul'**, that proceeds the upward, vertical ascension of the Spirit. Indeed, the descent (tanzil, which also means 'revelation') of the Qur'an is with a view to the eventual 'ascension' of the believers from this world to the celestial abodes, which is what the process of salvation (najah) involves. For the contemplatives of Islam, the Ascension of the Prophet was the prototype of the mystic's own spiritual ascension to Allah via that ray of the Spirit connecting his soul to the Divinity, with the practice of Nam of the living Master" (Victor Danner. The Islamic Tradition; p 48)

The Emigration (Hijrah)

'The year 620 was marked by a double personal tragedy for Muhammad, with the death of his wife, Khadijah and his uncle, Abu Talib. Khadijah had been the first to accept his Prophethood, and she had been his constant support and confidante, someone with whom he could share his concerns. Abu Talib had raised him from a small boy and, in the more troubled times of recent years, had protected him from the hostility of his tribe. Deprived of their protection and support, Muhammad found himself increasingly threatened by the powerful Quraysh.

Some 400 or so kilometres to the north of Mecca lay the Oasis town of Yathrih. The town was inhabited by several tribes — two of which were Arabs, the rest Jewish — who were constantly warring with each other. A number of people from Yathrib had come into contact with Muhammad and his teachings and, during the pilgrimage to the Ka'ba in 621, they met him on a mountain pass outside Mecca. Over the next few months, more Yathibrites adopted the teachings of the Prophet. In 622, at the 'second treaty of the pass', Muhammad and his Meccan followers were invited to migrate to Vathrib, where they would be given protection. Shortly afterwards the Meccan Muslims began to slip away to *Yathrib*.

By September, the only Muslims remaining in Mecca were Muhammad and his closest companions. They, too, were ready to leave. The Quraysh were determined to stop them. To evade his persecutors Muhammad left Mecca and headed south, in the opposite direction to Yathrib, accompanied by Abu Bakr, one of his oldest and closest followers. The two men hid for three days in a have on Mount Thawr; an hour's journey to the south of Mecca; until the hue and cry caused by their escape had abated. They then headed north to Yathrib, where in the months following Muhammad's arrival the first Islamic community *(ummha)* was formed. In time the town came to be known by another name: *madinat al-nabi*, or Medina, "*the City of the Prophet*" as city of temples ideology.

'The year (622) in which the emigration (hijrah) to Medina took place became the starting point of the Muslim lunar calendar = Surya Race Ka History, God and man— *Anno Hijarae* (AH). It is an appropriate point at which to interrupt the flow of historical events and open the Qur'an (*History of Chamar Dynasty*) and see the whole history of Dalit tribe of Quraysh = old concept, New Concept = Dalit or Gargotra tribe of Tehsil Akhnoor.

Note: "The Practical Reading and Writings" = Dharma Trust ke Story of **"Kashmir History"** = Prophet Mohammed = Dr. Shasnam Grewal ke inspiration + idiot Samaj of the Jammu and Kashmir state = great **Manmukhes** and after 71 years have been gone out of independence, they could not prove The "History of Dalit literature" = Islamic Concept. (Ruqaiyyah Maqsood; Islam; pp. 1-168) Note: The modern society of India including **Hindus, Christians, Muslims,** they have been trapped into illusion = snake value + animal culture = prostitution methods. (Ibid; p. 168). I+s+lam = Ego surrendered before the God = Lam study = Aksar Value = infinite knowledge = there is no Dananiti = torturing study of the Dalit History and literature. (Barack Obama; Speech on 8 Nov. 2011 Dr. Danraj Dahat; Ambedkar and his writings; pp. 1-172 Dr Raj Kumar = Animal culture of the political Era (1919-2017).

Chapter - 2

Jammu and Kashmir State: Geo-political Overview

Part - Two

Jammu and Kashmir State is strategically and geographically important due to its sensitive and central location. It was very difficult to demarcate the absolute geographical boundaries of the state due to mountainous topography. Credit goes to the Maharaja Gulab Singh - the first Dogra King - who took initiative to demarcate the territories, extending them from the river Ravi in the East to the river Indus in the West, as laid down by the Treaty of Amritsar on 16th of March, 1846. A.D. between the British East India Company and Gulab Singh, Maharaja of Jammu and Kashmir, (for more detail see appendix 2). Before 1846, Jammu, Kashmir and Ladakh were three separate regions and were under the control of different rulers of the areas.

Historical Background

Jammu

The name of Jammu city has been derived from the ruler of the area - *Jambu Lochan*. He was the ruler of the Bahu state across river Tawi along with his brother Bahu Lochan. Once, Raja Jambu Lochan came for hunting in the area west of river Tawi, he saw a Lion and Lamb drinking water together at a water tank. King was surprised and gave up the idea of hunting. He realised the importance and piousness of the place where the "lion" and the "lamb" took water together. He built a city around the tank. The city of Jammu was developed and named Jambudvipa. Later on, it was known as "Jammu". After the construction of Jammu city, the king Bahu Lochan constructed a fort on the eastern bank of the river Tawi and became the ruler of that area. It is said that Jammu city was founded about three thousand years ago (*Early History of Jammu Regionl;* pp. 1-100.)

Kashmir

The historical background of Kashmir is based upon interrupted series of written records (Note: Study the book of the author; **Prophet Mohd and his Teaching** for The Verification of dates) reaching back beyond the Islamic conquest of Sind 712 A.D. Some of the important sources of history of Kashmir are *Rajataringini* by poet *Kalhana* comprising of 8 cantos of Sanskrit written in the year 1148 A.D. as well as the statement of R.S. Tripathi about the 'Rai Dynasty of Sind, they ruled 137 years in Kashmir.' (History of Ancient India: pp.336-338) and Prophet had good relation with Kashmir through "*Arabian Sea* and Kayashap Rishi was the founder of the "**Kashmir History"** = OBC ka rule = Dera Bias ke History, before 1947 to modern man. (Dr. Raj Kumar; **"Ancient History of Kashmir";** pp. 1-20)*."*

The prevalent legend in Kashmir states that the valley was once covered by a huge lake on which Goddess Parvati sailed in a pleasure boat from Haramukh Mountain in the north to the Konsarnag Lake in the south. In her honour, the Lake was called as the "Satisar" or "Lake of the virtuous woman." The countryside was harassed by a demon popularly known as Jaldeo, a corruption of Jalodbhava. The grandson of Brahmaji, Kasyapa Rishi came to rescue, but for some time the demon eluded him, hiding under the water. Then, Vishnu interfered and struck the mountains at Baramulla with his trident. The waters of the lake rushed out, but the demon took refuge in the low ground near where now Srinagar situates, and baffled pursuit. Then, Parvati cast a mountain known as Hari Parbat, and from ancient times, the goddess has been worshipped on its slopes. When the demons had been routed, men visited the valley in the summer; and as climate became milder, they remained for also the winter. Little kingdoms sprang up and the little kings quarreled among themselves, with the usual result that a bigger king was called in to rule the country.

The celebrated poet-historian of Kashmir - Kalhana suggests that the political history of Kashmir originated with king Gonanda I, but most of the recent historians begin their studies with Ashoka, who lived in the third century B.C. A constant flow of invasions and dynastic erruptions which brought to power ruling families was the central feature of the succeeding two thousand years like Karkota and Loharas (600). The first Muslim rulers— Shah Mir ascended the throne in 1342 A.D. The rulership passed on from the Shah Mir family to the Chaks, who were Shias and came from the country of the Dards. Gazi Khan was the first Chak Ruler in 1554. In 1586, the Emperor Akbar defeated the Chaks, conquered the valley and made Srinagar his summer resort. Mughals ruled over Kashmir more than a century and a half.

Ahmed Shah Abdali conquered Kashmir. From that time, about 70years Kashmir was ruled by Afghans or Pathans, through Governors appointed by the king of Kabul.

In 1819, Maharaja Ranjit Singh of Punjab invaded Kashmir and was successful in wresting Kashmir from the Pathan rulers. For nearly 25 years, Kashmir was ruled by governors appointed by the Sikh Darbar at Lahore.

Ladakh

The word 'Ladakh' has been derived from Tibetian word La-Tags: *La* means pass and *Tags* means Mountains. Thus, it further means a land of passes and mountains. It is also referred as Mar-Yul (low land or Red land) and Kha-Cha-Pa or snow land. Both these names were used by Fahein who calls the kingdom as Kiechha and by Hwan-Tsang, who calls it *Ma-lo-pho* (Sindharra). (Ladakh and its Buddist Philosophy = **"A Complete History of J&K State."** (pp. 215-248 by Dr. Raj Kumar).

The history of Ladakh is intimately connected with Tibet. It is also referred to "*Little Tibet*" = the story of Father and son in the official records of the State. Leh is the capital of Ladakh which is known as the highest city located at 12,000 ft. at sea level. About the end of the 17th century, the Ladakh was ruled by the Sokpos - Mughal tribe (Dr. Raj Kumar **"Medieval History of Sudra";** pp. 518-578)). On the request of the Ladakhis, the governor of Kashmir provided the help to repel the Sokpos from Ladakh. Prior to the annexation by the Dogras, the government of the country was a mild form of monarchy. The ruler was called Gialpo or king, but the real power vested with the minister of Kahlon. Ladakh has been a tributaiy for centuries. About the middle of the 17th century, in 1687, the Mughals with the help of the rulers of the Western Tibet defected the Mughals and for nearly acentury, it remained with the Mongol. In 1834A.D. Gulab Singh, the ruler of Jammu, sent Zorawar Singh with a force of about 800 to conquer Ladakh. The king of Ladakh submitted agreeing to pay a war indemnity of Rs. 50,000/- so Gulab Singh became Raja of Ladakh also. He conquered Lhasa in 1842 and at the same time annexed Shardu and Baltistan. (*History* *of Ladakh*) study of Namgyal Dynasty by Dr. P.S. Jina, Central Institute of Buddhist Studies Leh (pp. 1-129).

Geo-Political Overviews of Jammu and Kashmir State

Jammu and Kashmir is a mountainous region. The State lies between 32° and 37°N and 73° and 80°E. The State has two capitals-the winter capital of the state, Jammu, lies in the South. Kashmir, the summer capital of the state, is situated in the central part at Chenani in Jammu region during the time of Dogra ruler (1847-1947). Gilgit is in the North and between the Kashmir Valley and Tibet is the province of Ladakh. The state has a population of 1.25 crore (12548926) which constitutes the 1.04% of the total population of India according to population 2011 census. The geo-political overview of the state can be understood through the following headings:

1. **Size or Area of the State:** The state of Jammu and Kashmir occupies an area of 222236 sq. kms. The territory of the state is under the control of three sovereign states i.e, India, Pakistan and China. India has occupied the territory of 101387 sq. kms. Whereas Pakistan occupied Kashmir measures about 748114 sq kms. An area of 37555 sq. kms. is occupied by China during 1962 war. An area of 5180 sq. kms under P.O.K. was handed over by Pakistan to China. Thus, China controls an area of 42735 kms of Kashmir territory.

   Jammu and Kashmir state is divided into three division namely Jammu, Kashmir and Ladakh with 22 districts, 56 sub-divisions/ districts, 265 tehsils, 370 Blocks, 3 municipalities, 3885 panchayats for administrative purposes and developmental activities.

   The Jammu region consists of 10 districts namely Kathua, Jammu, Samba, Udhampur, Reasi, Rajouri, Poonch, Doda, Ramban and Kishtwar.

   The Kashmir region consists of 10 districts namely Anantnag, Kulgam. Pulwama, Shopian, Budgam, Srinagar, Ganderbal, Bandipora, Baramulla and Kupwara.

   The Ladakh region consists of 2 districts namely Kargil and Leh.

   Jammu and Kashmir State has 221 kms in Jammu International Border with Pakistan region and 365 kms with China in its Ladakh region.The line of Control, (LOC) which divides India and POK of the State, is 1001 kms long.

The state is located in the Northern part of India. It shares border with Punjab and Himachal Pradesh to the South, Pakistan to the West, and Afghanistan to the North and China to the North-East.

2. **Physiographical Divisions:** Three regions of the state are different in topography. The valley of Kashmir is separated from Jammu region through the Pir Panchal range. Banihal Tunnel is the only connecting link by road between Jammu and Kashmir regions. Ladakh and Kashmir regions are joined by a route through Zojila Pass of the Great Himalayas. These three regions can be understood as physiographical divisions in the following three ways.

1. **Sub-Himalayas Jammu:** This sub-Himalayan Jammu division is further classified into three categories:

(1) The Outer Plains

(2) The Shivaliks

(3) The Middle Himalayas

(1) The Outer Plains; The outer plains lie towards the southern part of the state. Its width is in 5-25 kms and it stretches from River Ravi to River Chenab for an extension of 110 kms. It spreads in the southern parts of Akhnoor called Jio Pota, R.S. Pura, Samba and Kathua. There are two hundred bridges on the Jammu Railway line in this region.

Inspite of Ravi and Chenab rivers, this plain region is drained by the Ujh, the Basantar, the Tawi and the Manawar Tawi. The waters of these rivers are used for irrigation purposes. These plains are highly fertile lands. Kathua, Hiranagar, Bishnah, R.S. Pura, Domana and Akhnoor are the productive crop lands.

(2) The Shivaliks Hills: The Shivaliks are also known as Jammu Hills in Jammu and referred as the Himalayan foot hills. They are also designated as "Outer Hills". They lie to the North of Jammu Plains for a distance of about 200 kms between the Ravi and the Jehlum rivers. The width of Shivaliks is between 20-25 kms. Jasrota, Akhnoor and Samba are the important towns of the Shivaliks. To the north of the Siwalik Hills lie a series of flat bottomed, wide longitudinal valleys, covered with thick gravel and alluvieum, called the *duns*. These *duns* provide sufficient land fit for ploughing. Udhampur, Kotli, Basholi Ramkote, Dansal and Sunderbani are the important *duns*. These areas are highly populated. There are famous lakes - *Mansar* and *Saruinsar*- in the Shivaliks hills.

The lower hill slopes of Shivaliks, with the thirsty soils having low water table and scarcity water, constitute above the "*Kandi*" areas of Ranbir canal and Partap canal and Rajputs Brahmin Basti of Maharaja Hari Singh = old sectt.

The winter capital of the Jammu and Kashmir state i.e. Jammu City, popularly known as "*City of Temples*", is situated at an altitude of 366 meters on the southern slope of Shivaliks, 32°.44' latitude and 74°.55' longitude, on the banks of river Tawi. The city is connected by a concrete bridge called as Tawi Bridge and a "Fly-Over".

(3) The Middle Himalayas: The middle Himalayas, locally known as *Pahar* (mountains) in Jammu region, spread between the Ravi in the east and Poonch in the west. The middle Himalaya region is famous for its scenic beauty and forest resources. It covers 1820 meters to 2240 meters, with a width of about 60 kms in the eastern parts of Jammu division and 10 kms near Rajouri. Ramnagar, Bhadrwaha, Kishtwar, Padder, Reasi, Thatri, Rajouri, Kud, Patnitop, Batote, Poonch and beyond to Muzzafrabad are the small valleys in this region.

Trikuta mountain is also situated in this region. The famous cave of Shri Mata Vaishno Devi is situated in one of the peaks of Trikuta Hills called Katra=Blind Faith Ke Theory = Brahminism Ka Dor + Meghwal ke **Bechti** (Insult) during the rule of capitalist society = old Hari - Singh ka rule. (Daily Ex. Article published by Parsotam Singh Mannas; p. 1st of the Sunday Mogazine).

Deodar (Oak), Blue-pine and Silver-fir are found in its higher altitudes. Both deciduous and scrub are the dominant species in its lower altitudes i.e., below 1800 meters. The Jammu-Srinagar National Highway has been carved out through the Mid-Himalayas, via Patnitop Pass, Batote, Ramban, Ramsoo, Banihal and Banihal pass Pir Panjal pass. This region has cool climate. The Pir Panjal representing the middle-Himalayan ranges consists of lofty mountains covering 3500 to 5000 meters.

2. Himalayan Kashmir: Kashmir Region can be understood with the help of following headings-

(1) The Kashmir Valley

(2) The Karewas

(3) The Side Valleys

(1) The Kashmir Valley: The Himalayan Kashmir is enclosed between the Great Himalayas in the North and the Pir Panjal in the South. Its location gives rise to an oval basin of Kashmir. The scenic and beautiful Kashmir Valley exposes its beauty beyond the 'Pir Panjal', after crossing the Banihal Tunnel, 2194.56 meters above the sea level. The valley is surrounded by tall and towering mountain chains on all sides except for certain passes and a narrow gorge at Baramulla, formed by the river Jehlum; between two parallel mountains- the Pir Panchal and the Kazi Nag. The river Jhelum leaves for its downward journey to the plains through this gorge.

The Kashmir Valley is surrounded by the mountains- the Nanga Parbat and Tosh Maidan in the north, and Mahadev, Gwash Brari and Shri Amarnath in the south; the Pir Panjal in the south-west and the Kazi Nag in the north-west and the Harmukh on the eastern side.

The valley region consists of famous meadows of Khilanmarg, Kongawattan, Gulmarg and Yusmarg.

The mountain rim around the valley is scattered with small mountain lakes such as Sheshnag and Gangabal in the Himalayas and Kousarnag and Alapathar in the Pir Panjal Range.

The National Highway from Jammu after crossing Banihal Pass through Jawahar Tunnel (2210 m) in the Pir Panchal range, passes through Qazikund, Khanabal, Bijbhera, Sangam, Chursoo, Avantipora, Barsoo, Letapora, Pampore, Panthachok and Panderthan. Its opposite side dominates the city of Srinagar from its north east corner. From the south-east side, the city is commanded by Shankracharya small rocky hill where the world famous Shankarcharya Temple is situated. The Hill is stretched as an arc bordering the famous Dal Lake

The deepest lake in Asia- The Wular Lake is located in the Baramulla district of the valley. Another Lake- the Mansabal Lake near to Ganderbal is famous for its scenic beauty and charming waters.

The winter capital of the State is Srinagar. This city is also known as the '*Venice of the East.*' It is located on 34°.5' latitude and 74°50' longitude, on the banks of the Jhelum from south east to north west. The Hari Prawat Hill, the famous Shrine Hazratbal, Shankracharya Temple and Dal Lake are in the centre of Srinagar city.

(2) The Karewas: The Karewas are the unique physical features of the Kashmir valley. They are fresh water deposits which are found as low flat mounds or elevated plateaus. There are two types of Karewas in Kashmir-

(1) The sloping Karewas

(2) The flat topped Karewas

(1) Sloping Karewas: These Karewas extend along the flanks of Pir Panjal range, Kulgam, Shopian, Charisharif, Damodar, Dud fathri, Gulmarg and Baramulla are the important sloping Karwas.

(2) Flat topped Karewas: These Karewas are found on the right bank of river Jhelum i.e. Mattan, Tral, Avantipora, Pampore, Safapora, Ganderbal, Bandipora and Handwara. Bijbhera and Payer Karewas lie on the left bank of river Jhelum.

(3) The Side Valleys: The side valleys consist of famous and side valley namely—

(1) Lidder Valley

(2) Sind Valley

(3) Lolab Valley

(4) Kishenganga Valley

(1) The Lidder Valley: The Lidder is an important tributary of the Jhelum river. It forms an upland valley in the east. The Lidder Valley opens into the south east end of the Kashmir Valley, giving passage to the Lidder river. It extends in the north direction to Pahalgam, a distance of about 35 kms from Kashmir valley. The holy Amarnath cave lies in this valley. The shortest route to follow from Pahalgam to Amarnath on foot or by ponies is Chandanwari, Pinshu Top, Zojapal, Sheshnag, Wavbal, Mahagonus top, Panchtarni and holy Amarnath cave.

(2) Sindh Valley: The Sindh Valley is the most famous side valley of Kashmir. It starts from Ganderbal and terminates at Zojila pass, which is the entry of Ladakh region. The National Highway from Srinagar to Leh leads through this valley. Kangan, Gund, Sonamarg, Baltal and Zojila areas are laid in this valley. The climate of the Sindh Valley is hard and harsh during winter. The Sindh river is frozen during winter.The Thajiwas and Hapatgund Glaciers are situated in 3 kms south of Sonamarg. This valley connects the Kashmir Valley with the Central Asia and with, modern Afghanistan. The later history of Sind is mainly of local interest.

We learn of internecine struggle and rise and fall of Arab principalities like "*Multan*" and "*Mansurah*". (R.S. Tripathi, pp. 338-339).

(3) **The Lolab Valley:** This valley is situated on the north-western side of Kashmir. This oval shaped valley is about 6.4 kms in length and 4.8 kms in width. It lies in the Kupwara district of Kashmir divisions. This valley is across the Pir Panjal. It is traversed by a stream called the Lolab.

(4) **The Kishenganga Valley:** This valley is formed by the famous tributary of river Jhelum - the Kishenganga. This river or the river of Krishna, rises in the eastern of the Tilail valley and flows westwards. It is joined by Raman Sindh from the south. After joining with Burzil stream, it bends in the north-west directions through the Gurez valley and Dawar areas. It has cold, hard and harsh climate.

(5) **Trans-Himalayan Ladakh:** Ladakh is the loftiest inhabited region of the world. It has majestic mountains, deep valleys, high plateau, towering peaks, vast table-lands, various rivers and green valleys. It comprises of cold deserts and desolated plateaus. The following are three main ranges of the Ladakh region:-

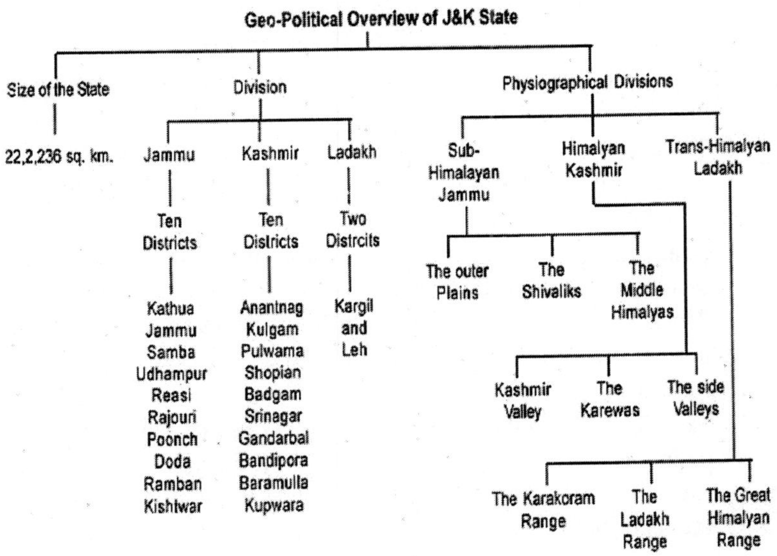

(1) The Karakoram Range: The KaraKoram or "*Black Mountains*" chain forms the natural boundary of Ladakh and the areas of Baltistan, Hunza-Nagar and Gilgit are in the north of Ladakh. The Karakoram lies towards North of Shyok with lofty peaks and vast glaciers. The Karakoram pass lies close to the source of river Shyok. The Karakoram mountains radiate from the Pamirs towards the north-east. While Aghil and Kunlun mountains extend towards China, and Hindukush towards Afghanistan. The Karakoram forms the watershed between Central Asia and South Asia. The total length of this range to the Shyok river to the Gilgit river is about400 kms. Siachin, Biafo, Hispar, Baltoro and Chogolungma are the important glaciers of the Karakoram Range.

(2) The Ladakh Range: The Ladakh range lies between the Indus river and its famous tributary Shyok. It touches the border with China and Tibet. It is about 350 kms long and 50 kms wide. It forms a famous range in the Trans-Himalayan region. It is a straight range with a north-west to south-east trend. This range contains 24 important mountain peaks in which 9 peaks exceed 6000 m and rest of the 15 peaks range between 5000-6000 m. Khardung La is the highest mountain pass of the world over which the motor vehicles ply. Chang La, Digar La, Chorbat and Tsaka La are another important mountain passes of this range. In addition to it, tourist visited Ladakh via Manali and Srinagar respectively.

Leh is the divisional headquarters of Ladakh. Leh is situated on the right bank of the Indus river. Leh has remained the historic "Silk route" from Singkiang to west Asia and to the plains of India. Leh is also known as the dust bowl of Kashmir and Buddhist learning centre.

Changthang-the home of Changpas or Champas-is situated on the eastern part of Ladakh. This plateau lies between the Ladakh and Zanskar ranges. It has hot springs in Pugga Valley an Chumanthang. It also has salt water lakes like Tsomoriri, Tsokhyagar and Rupshu.

(3) The Great Himalayan Ranges: The Great Himalayan ranges including Zanskar range are situated in the northern side of the Kashmir valley. The Nanga Prabat stands in the western end near the Indus bend of this range. The Nanga Parbat is its highest peak attaining an elevation of 8126 m. Ruberung La, Sersank Pass, Poat La, Umasi La, Singo La, Sir Sir La, Lanak La, Bara Lacha La, Burjila, Rohtang Pass, Kanzam La, Chilung La, Fotu La, and

Zojila are the important passes of this range = Backward culture. The Zanskar range is located at an altitude of 5940 m and famous for its two river valleys namely the Zanskar and Suru. *Padam* is the population area of the Zanskar Valley. It has cold weather due to heavy snow fall on the Pensila pass.

The famous Kargil town is located in the Suru valley with an altitude of 2676. Another important town of Suru valley is Drass. Drass is the second inhabited coldest place in the world after Siberia having-50° Celsius in winter. The Dards and Balties inhabit the Suru and Zanskar valleys.

The National Highway from Srinagar to Leh Crosses the Zanskar range through two mountain passes i.e. Namki La and Fatu La.

Geo-political Features of Jammu and Kashmir are responsible for the emergence of identity politics in all the three regions—*Jammu, Kashmir* and *Ladakh.* These features have developed in each region its distinct and aggressive political identity which have led towards divergent political aspirations without bothering about the interests of the other two regions, that is of Dera Bias and Jammu state (Punjab and Delhi).

Note: After the enforcement of J&K constitution in 1957 to till today, the state politics has been revolving around the identity politics = Dalit Studies or Chamar thought = New Study of the Tribal Culture. This state is highly plural in its socio-political and geographical context. So as far as its social diversity is concerned, Kashmir has the most population of the Sunni Muslims with minority of Shia. They form a distinct group and differentiate themselves from other Muslims of the state. The Ladakhi - speaking Shia Muslims of the Kargil also form a separate tribal identity as the Gujjars and Pahari Muslims do. Gujjars give importance to their tribal identity and even claim themselves to be the third largest group of the state after the Kashmiri Muslims and the Hindus of Jammu. On the other hand, the Hindus of the Jammu are also internally differentiated themselves on the basis of their caste, cultural and linguistic categorization. Kashmiri Pandits feel culturally close to Kashmiri Muslims as compared to Dogra Hindus. Dalits form a distinct category as opposed to Upper caste Hindus, mostly Rajput-Brahmins and Mahajans of the Jammu region on the basis of social justice.

The social diversity has given birth to the multiple identity politics which can be understood under the following headings:-

1. Kashmiri Identity Politics = Negative Approach or Era of Rites and Rituals.

2. Regional Identity Politics = Development of the human History.
3. Tribal Identity Politics = Chamar thought
4. Sub-Regional Identity Politics = Co-relative theory of "Sudra Family".

1. **Kashmiri Identity Politics =** Negative approach.**:** It is visible at national and international level, as the story of God and man
2. **Regional Identity Politics = Development of the Human History :** Regional identity politics can be seen in other two regions i.e. in "*Jammu and Ladakh*". This politics is based on power ideology and distribution of resources within the state.The state politics revolves around the distribution of the state resources like educational and employment opportunities. Development of infrastructure facilities etc. Due to these differences, here arises the demand for Union Territory Status for Ladakh and demand for "*Jammu State*".
3. **Tribal Identity Politics =** Chamar thought**:** It is based on the politics of God of the marginal groups like Gujjars Bakarwah and Dalits of the state. These groups are located in the peripheral areas of Jammu. These are targeting the educational and employment opportunities provided by the state. They are engaged in competitive identity politics = Sudra State of mind.
4. **Sub-Regional Identity Politics = Co-relative theory of Sudra Family :** The people residing in the remote border belt of Poonchh-Rajouri and the underdeveloped areas of the Doda belt feel neglected and alienated by the regional politics of Jammu, Kashmir and Ladakh. Therefore, they demand for Peer -Panchal Hill Council for the Poonch-Rajouri districts and Chenab Valley Hill Council for Doda belt respectively.

   Similarly, in Ladakh, there are Leh Development Hill Council for Ladakhis and Kargil Development Hill Council for Muslims in the Ladakh region.

Note:- Before the Dogra State, there was a disintegration of the empire and Lord Dalhousie United this state on the bases of common culture = Dalit Christan. Hari Singh is proved Brahmins of the modern period and his son Dr. Karan Singh and his two sons as neglected rules of this area MLA and MP as old Brahmins of the Nepal territory = migratory race of the original tribe called Brahmin-Rajput.

Chapter - 3

Formation of Jammu and Kashmir State = Old View and New Ideology = Chamar thought; Past and Present or Infinite Knowledge

Jammu was ruled by a Dogra Chief of the Rajput named Ranjit Deo in the middle of the 18th century. He died in 1780 A.D. and a struggle was begun among his three grand nephews-Gulab Singh, Dhiyan Singh and Suchet Singh. They were the sons of Kishore Singh. The dispute among them gave an opportunity to the Sikh Darbar of Lahore to capture the kingdom of Jammu. Jammu was annexed to the Sikh territory in 1808 and three sons of Kishore Singh took services under Raja Ranjit Singh.

Ranjit Singh accompanied by Gulab Singh and his great General Misr Dewan Chand defeated the then Governor of Kashmir Jabar Khan in 1819. Kashmir passed on the hands of Sikhs after five generations of Muslim rule. Maharaj Ranjit Singh acknowledged Gulab Singh as the Maharaja of Jammu. He performed the Raj Tilak of Gulab Singh under a tree of Jiyapota located on the banks of rives Chinab near Akhnoor town on 17th November, 1820. He had given the area of Bhimber and Chibal including Poonch to Dhiyan Singh and Ram Nagar to Suchet Singh. Both Dhiyan Singh and Suchet Singh were killed in the Nam - History = story of birth and rebirth and their jagirs also fell in the hands of Gulab Singh as the story of modern Sabita of Raj Rishi = Gulab Singh + Dalit literature + Baba Gurinder Singh of Panjab = Free Squad as Missionary leaders = Radha Soami Dera Bias (Nazwal Jammu).

Gulab Singh captured and conquered Rajouri and Kishtwar in 1821. He also fought against his own clansman, Mian Dido Jamwal, who led a rebellion against the Sikhs. He was executed by Maharaja Gulab Singh.

Why because of the incomplete knowledge of the subject **"History"** = Story of God and Man. In this way, he conquered one by one different places and regions of the state like Jammu, Poonch, Ram Nagar, Basohli, Kishtwar, Bhimbar, Bhaderwah, Rajouri, Sikardu, Kharmang, Kiris, Khaplu, Sheghar, Astor Gilgit, Chitral Yasin, Hunza, Nagar and Punial.

P.N.K. Bamzai writes, '*Maharaja Gulab Singh'* is the only Indian ruler to have carved out a state during the 19th century out of the wreckage of the great kingdom of Sikhs. Moreover, he was the only Indian ruler to have extended the frontiers of India to their natural boundary." (pp. 1-40)

Maharaja Gulab Singh extended the boundaries of Jammu to Western Tibet with the help of General Zorawar Singh. General Zprawar Singh has been referred as the '*Napoleon of India*' by the British historians. Zorawar Singh was the Governor of Kishtwar who conquered the Suru valley and Kargil (1835), the rest of Ladakh in 1836-40 and Baltistan 1840.

After the death of Maharaj Ranjit Singh of Punjab, in 1839 A.D, the government at Lahore was not in a good condition = Dirty politics. There was wild anarchy all over the state. Gulab Singh was the commander-in-chief at that time (B.L. Grover and Grover; pp 147-153).

Lord Hardinge declared a war against the Sikhs in 1845 A.D. only to eliminate the Sikh rule in Punjab. An Anglo-Sikh war broke out between the British and the Sikhs at Sobraon in November, 1845 in which Gulab Singh was not interested to help the Sikhs. He wanted to earn the gratitude of the British diplomats in order to establish his own state. After becoming the Prime-Minister of Punjab, he remained in touch with the British authorities.

The Sikh army was defeated in 1846 A.D. The English occupied Lahore on 20th February 1846. Raja Gulab Singh appeared on the scene as a mediator between the English and the Lahore Darbar.

The Treaty of Lahore was concluded between the defeated Sikhs i.e. Raja Dalip Singh of Lahore and the British on 9th March 1846 (See Appendix 1) in which the British demanded rupees one and a half crore as a war indemnity (Also see '*A Modern History of Untouchables'*, unpublished material). The British kept this kind of demand only to weaken the Sikh Darbar. Maharaj Dalip Singh of Lahore ceded to the East India Company, in perpetual sovereignty, all his forts, territories and rights in the Doab and country, hill or plain, situated between river Beas and Satluj." (see appendix 1 article 3) Moreover, this treaty also stated that the Maharaja (Dalip Singh) hereby agreed to recognize the independent sovereignty of Raja Gulab Singh in such territories Lord Dalhosue and Sikh wars. (See appendix 1 article 12 and 13)

Maharaja Dalip Singh was not in a position to pay a heavy amount because he was on death bed. Inspite of that, he ceded all his territories from the Beas river to the Indus, including J&K but for certain administrative and other difficulties. Lord Hardinge considered the occupation of the whole of this territory in adviceable. Raja Gulab Singh was ready and claimed this track as his hereditary possession. He offered to pay the war indemnity on the condition that he was made the independent ruler of Jammu and Kashmir State.

However, Treaty of Amritsar was concluded on 16th March, 1846 between the British Government and Raja Gulab Singh at Amritsar. The Treaty of Amritsar 1846 has laid down the foundation of Jammu and Kashmir. Article 3 of this treaty states,

"In consideration of the transfer made to him and his heir by the provision of the foregoing Articles, Maharaja Gulab Singh will pay to the British Government the sum of 75 lakhs of rupees (*Nanakshahi*) fifty lakhs to be paid on ratification of this Treaty and twenty-five lakhs on or before the 1st October of the current year of 1846 A.D."

With the signing of Treaty of Amritsar in 1846, Maharaja Gulab Singh became the ruler of Jammu and Kashmir on the basis of his work and achievements. In this way, the Jammu and Kashmir state was formed by Maharaja Gulab Singh.

Note: Maharaja Gulab Singh was helpless at that time and he noticed to Afgani ruler Dost Mohammad to sign a pact with Lord Dalhosie (1848-56), on the question of that this state will ruled by the Pahari Dalit rulers as Nams on earth from Gulab Singh to Maharaja Pratap Singh. (B.L. Grover and Alaka Grover; pp. 147-153), **"A New Look on Modern India."**

Chapter - 4

Political Awakening in Kashmir

K.S. Sexsana ke Kitab (Published in 1973 Foreword by Dr. Karan Singh Brahmin - Rajput).

Jammu And Kashmir State was ruled by the autocratic rule of the Dogra Maharajas. During Maharaja's rule, land reform programmes were benefitted by the land owners of the Jammu province and not to the Kashmir valley. All Kashmiris were not recruited in the military services. Even Kashmiri peasantry found itself shouldering the heaviest burdens of the state government's unfair policies and taxes etc = Mehbooba Mufti + Dr. Farooq ke Govt..

Youngmen's Muslim Association: A Religious and Social Organization of Muslims was established as **Youngmen's Muslim Association in 1909** and Reform Act of the same year in Jammu by Malik Maqbool Ahmed Munshi, Mohd. Basharat, Qazi Shams-ud-din, Mirza Feroze-ud-din etc. It was very popular association and started looking at it for Political Organization as opposition group of Dr. B.R. Ambedkar (Mahar). But its leaders were accommodated with job and services by the Maharaja. Thus, it became totally failure to prove the Dalit History and Literature; even after 71 years of independence.

Reading Room Party: There was no political organistion for political discussion about the grievances of the people when Sheikh Mohd. Abdullah returned to Kashmir after completing his education form Aligarh in April 1930. He opened a Reading Room in a house at Srinagar on 9th May 1930. It was a place for books and newspapers reading but inside the room, the gathered youth used to discuss the current political affairs of the Maharaja rule. With the passage of time, it became the rallying point and centre of intellectual Kashmir youth; modern Kashmir University who began to think for the formation of political plateform for the protection of the oppressed people of the state called as Dalit Mislums = Present study of the Brahminmat of Kashmir.

In 1931, a number of speeches delivered by Abdul Quadeer to the Muslims in the mosque of Shah Hamdan in Srinagar and later on his arrest, a scuffle occurred between the Muslim mob and the state Armed Forces outside the jail. This incident encouraged the people of Kashmir to organize themselves against the autocratic and tyrannical rule of Maharaja.

The Maharaja Hari Singh appointed a Glancy Commission under the chairmanship of Sir B. J. Glancy on 12th November, 1931 to find out the grievances and complaints of the different communities ad sections of the state. This commission recommended the abolition of the Malikana, the grazing taxes, relaxation of rules regarding cultivation of state owned waste lands, the right of the owner to cut walnut, Chinar and mulberry trees from their lands, fairshare in the state services etc.

Birth of Muslim Conference = Brahmin Missionary Race

Glancy Commission had sown the seeds of formation of Muslim Conference as a first political organization to present the people's grievances. Sheikh Mohd. Abdullah and his associates took the initiate in the Reading Room for the birth of the '*Political Organization*'. Three-days long discussion was held at the Pather Masjid at Zainakadal on 15th-1 7th October 1932. Near about three lacs people attended this convetion. All Jammu and Kashmir Muslim Conference was established under the president ship of Sheikh Mohd. Abdullah. It was the first political party of the State.

From 1932-1938, there were six annual sessions of the party. Four sessions were held in Srinagar, Mirpur, Jammu and Poonch were presided over by Sheikh Mohd. Abdullah. Third and fourth sessions were held in Sopore and Srinagar. These sessions were presided over by Mian Ahmed Yar and Chowdhary Ghulam Abbas respectively.

The working Committee of the Muslim Conference demanded a New Constitution and an Assembly. It observed 8th May 1936 as a Responsible Government Day.

Transformation of APP Jammu and Kashmir Muslim Conference into All Jammu and Kashmir National Conference

Sheikh Mohammad Abdullah was very much influenced by the great leaders of India National Congress especially Mahatma Gandhi and Pt. Jawahar Lal Nehru as well as the state leaders like Prem Nath Bajaj, Sardar Budh Singh, Kashap Bandhu. He also realized the support of non-muslim community of state for their independence. He started thinking in terms of secularism. (See the book of the author (Novel) '*Doda city and Drug Addition'*.

For it, a meeting of the working committee of the All Jammu and Kashmir Muslim Conference was held on 28th June, 1938 to move a suggesting to change the name of the conference to National Conference and to amend the constitution so as to 'throw its doors open' to non-Muslims. The resolution was passed by a majority of 17 against 3 votes. Due to the change in the name, the All Jammu and Kashmir National Conference opened the doors for the Hindus and Sikhs for the national struggle for the historical reaseach as Nam on earth.

The National Conference observed 5th August, 1938 as the Responsible Government Day - The All Jammu and Kashmir National Conference became a formal member of the all India State People's Conference in 1941 with affiliations in most princely states as new idea of Dalit literature. Sheikh Mohd. Abdullah was the elected President of the all India states People's Conference in 1946. He established a close contact with the Indian National Congress leader Pt. Jawahar Lal Nehru. His association strengthened the nationalistic policies of the National Conference in Kashmir and Jammu.

New (Naya) Kashmir Manifesto

After the renamed of Muslim Conference as National Conference, people belonged to different sections were allowed to join the struggle against the autocratic rule of the Maharaja. Sheikh Abdullah along with his liberal progressive non-Muslim friends like Kashyap Bandhu, Jia Lal Kilam, Pandit Sudama Sidha, Prem Nath Bazaz and Sardar Budh Singh drafted the National Demands the forerunner of the famous Naya Kashmir (New Kashmir) Manifesto, which was a Charter of demands for granting a Democratic Constitution committed to the welfare of the common people of Kashmir *(A Complete History of Jammu and Kashmir State by Dr. Raj Kumar)*.

Its annual session was held at Sopore in Kashmir on 29th-30th September 1944.

The delegates to this session unanimously approved a Manifesto '*New Kashmir*' as the objective of the National Conference. Its Preamble states, "***We The People Of Jammu, Kashmir, Ladakh And The Frontier Regions, Including Poonch And Chinani Ilaqas*** -commonly known as ***Jammu And Kashmir State***-in order to perfect our Union in the fullest equality and self-determination, to raise ourselves and our children forever from the abyss of oppression and poverty, degradation and superstition from medieval darkness and ignorance, into the Sunlit valleys of plenty ruled by freedom of conscience ad honest toil, in worthy participation of the historic resurgence of the people of the East and the working masses of the world, and in determination to make this our country a dazzling gem upon the snowy bosom of Asia, ***Do Propose And Propound The Following Constituion Of Our State.***"

The New Kashmir Manifesto was divided into two parts—

(A) The Constitution of Jammu and Kashmir State

(B) The National Economic Plan.

The part of dealing with the constitution of the state was further sub-divided into several sections including—

1. Citizenship (J&K State)
2. The National Assembly (Brahminism)
3. The Ruler (Labour Party)
4. The Council of Ministers (Dalits)
5. Justice (Patwari)
6. Local Administration (Sarpanch)
7. The National Language (Hindi & English)

1. Citizenship: The second, deals with citizenship, guarants the peoples of Jammu and Kashmir—

(a) Freedom of the speech
(b) Freedom of the press
(c) Freedom of assembly and meetings
(d) Freedom of strict processions and demonstration freedom of conscience
(e) Freedom of worship (Radha Soami = Nam or Kalma)

It also guaranteed socio-economic rights to the citizens of Jammu and Kashmir such as -

(a) Right to work (Dalit History)
(b) Right to rest (Patient Quality)
(c) Right to receive education for all students
(d) Scholarship provision for deserving poor students
(e) Equal rights for women
(f) Special protection to the interests of mother and child through law etc.

2. The National Assembly: The manifesto also required that the National Assembly, the highest legislature of the state, should be elected by citizens of the State by electoral districts on the basis of one deputy per 40,000 persons, for a period of five years.

3. The Ruler: The Ruler would enjoy the constitutional status in the state. (Gargotra tribe)

4. The Council of Ministers: The Council of Ministers of the State should be responsible to the National Assembly. Section 27 of the manifesto stated the position of Ruler to-be reduced to that of the Constitutional Head. (Dalit Samaj ke Cabinet)

5. Justice: Naya or New Kashmir Manifesto provided the independence of the judiciary with the constitution of the High Court and Peoples court at District and Tehsil levels. It stated that the Judges of the High Court Would be elected by the Assembly for a period of five years. The Peoples Courts judges were to be elected by the Panchayats and the High Court empowered to supervise and direct the judicial functions of such Subordinate Courts.

6. Planned Economy: This Manifesto also provided Planned Economy which was further sub-divided into the following-

(a) Production (God Human Souls)
(b) Transport (Cars and Mini Bus)
(c) Distribution (Knowledge)
(d) Utility Services (Govt. Salary)
(e) Currency and Finance

It also ensured for the organization of agriculture on modern and rational footing providing higher standard of living for the peasants. It promised to the abolition of landlordism and distribution of land to the tiller. The agriculture plan was promised to take into consideration for national self-sufficiency in essential foodstuffs and crops.

7. The National Languages: According to Naya Kashmir Manifesto, the national languages of the state would be Kashmiri, Dogri, Balti, Dardi, Punjabi, Hindi and Urdu. Urdu would be a mixture of several languages of the state.

Note:- It is like the Quit Indian Movement of Mahatma Gandhi and P.N. Bazaz to spread the message of new Chinese state about the history of 'Hindu Civilization' or China as the story of thinking to rethinking of Baba

Gurinder Singh and his daughter Miss Ramiyan Bhardwaj & Prof. Renu *Angurana ke Soch* and implementation of the Dalit History in Jammu and Kashmir State. (Dalit Studies and Chamar thought;" by Dr. Raj Rishi; unpublished material).

Chapter - 5

Political Awakening in Jammu = Advocate Meher Chand Mahajan ke Soch

Note: The political awakening in the Kashmir Valley in 1931 under the leadership of Sheikh Mohammad Abdullah due to the economic unrest created a sense of political awakening in the Jammu region also. The activities of the All Jammu and Kashmir National Conference was proved failure to take the support of the Jammu region especially the Hindu dominated belts. Its genesis, growth and ideological moorings made it a suspect in the eyes of the Dogra Nationalists of Jammu, who looked upon it as something alien and totally unacceptable. The Hindus of Jammu wanted to continue rule over Kashmir. Sheikh Abdullah's anti-Dogra bias and the Quit Kashmir Movement of 1946 made the National Conference an organization with no appeal for the Jammu Hindus, The Jammu Hindus considered NC as an organization for eliminating their influence from Kashmir.

Maharaja Hari Singh left the Kashmir Valley on 26th October, 1947 in the wake of the tribal attack = Gujarat feelings (Rohit Culture) and came to Jammu. He decided to leave the state on health ground. Thus, he appointed his Yuvraj Karan Singh as Regent with all powers and functions with regards to the state. It developed a feeling of insecurity in the minority community Dalit Hindus and Muslims. The aggressive trends in the Kashmiri nationalism and fear of political power passing into the hands of Kashmiri Muslims made the Dogras of Jammu politically ignoraned and condemned. Sheikh Abdullah's revolutionary plans for economic and social changes as mentioned in the New Kashmir Manifesto bad challenged and affected the economic interests of the majority of the people in the Jammu region. They believed in the great security within the India Union and this, demanded full integration of the state with India. As a result, a movement was launched against Sheikhs Mohammad Abdullah and his party All Jammu and Kaslimir National Conference. Later on, the movement took the shape of a political party called as the Praja Parishad as the story of "*Hindu Rakashas Sena*" and his head is called Salinder Singh Jamwal. (History Deptt. University of Jammu and Colleges study centre).

Praja Parishad

The Praja Parishad came into existence in November, 1947 and a group of R.S.S. workers took a leading part in its formation. Hari Wazir was the first President of the party. Balraj Madhok was its General Secretary Hari Wazir was succeeded by Lala Roop Chand Nanda. The party gained strength with the adhesion of such leaders like Prem Nath Dogra and others. Very soon, it became the only representative party of the Jammu Hindus. It also became the Principal Opposition Party of Jammu and the local instrument of its protest. The *Praja Parishad* became excellent organistation in 1951. It had whole time workers. It was strengthened by the main local influential Hindus as Ganga Ram, Nishchint Singh, Rattan Singh, the former I.G.P, Janak Singh etc. Moreover, it had close touch with the Hindu Mahasabha,the Ram Rajya Parishad and Jan Sangh. (as Dalit's story building measure)

"The Praja Parishad" sought security in the retention of the Institution of the Maharaja as a Constitutional Head of the State it favoured closer ties between the State and the Indian Union and abrogation of Article 370. It rejected a Separate Assembly, Separate Emblem and Separate Flag for the State and the Institution of *Sadar-I-Riyasat*. It demanded the application of the Indian constitution in its entirety = Nakama Adami Dr. Karan Singh.

It policy was influenced by the ideology of the "*Akhand Bharat*" and regarded the accession of the State to Union as final, complete, legally valid and beyond question. The party believed in the concept of India as a strong Unitary State as modern view of the National History.

The Praja Parishad started an agitation against the N.C. on the following grounds:-

1. National Conference had tried to muslimize the state in the name of secularism. Its almost first official act after coming in power was to split up the Hindu majority district of Udhampur in Jammu into two by lumping together Bhadrwah at, Kisthwar and Ramban areas of that district into a new Muslim majority district of Doda;
2. There had been totalitarianism in the name of democracy. Nomination papers of 44 of the 59 candidates of the Praja parishad had been scrapped on flimsy grounds;
3. Civil liberties had been attacked;

4. Steps had been taken towards the creation of an Independent Kashmir. The cult of Kashmiri Nationalism as against Indian nationalism had been preached;
5. The Delhi Agreement was betrayal. (For more details of Delhi Agreement, 1952 see appendix 3)

In its earlier stage, the Praja Parishad was not in the favour of Assembly to draft Separate Constitution for the State. Later on, it decided to contest the elections and demanded representation in Delimitation Committee. Soon after the party leadership charged the N.C. It boycotted the elections under protest. It raised the slogan—

"Ek Desh Mein Do Vidhan

Ek Desh Mein Do Nishan

Ek Desh Mein Do Pradhan

Nahih Chalenge! Nahih Chalenge!"

In one country Two Constitutions

In one country Two Flags

In one Country Two Prime-ministers = complete concept of New India or State = study the article of **Siyasat Nama** or Idea of the Welfare state.

Will not be tolerated = One Agenda = Anti – Dalit Propaganda.

A minor incident over the protest of a few students against hoisting a National Conference Flag in G.G.M. Science College, Jammu on 15th January 1952 added fuel to the fire. This incident disturbed the students by hunger strike, violence, police lathi-charge firing, partial paralisation of administrative machinery in Jammu city, intervention of the Military and imposition of 72 hours curfew. The entire leadership of the Praja Parishad was arrested as the Government charged that the demonstration was organization and inspired by the Praja Parishad. Later on, in April 1952, all were released with the intervention of Mr. N.G. Ayyanger, the then Minister of State of India. He took the initiative and studied the situation with cool passions.

Dogra Sadar Sabha, Jammu = Old Record; New Record = Kalhana" Rajatarangini

Dogra Sadar Sabha, Jammu is the oldest democratic, secular and social organization of the region, now it is called Raj-Rishi ke Sabita. It was established before independence in 1904 A.D. under the patronage of Mahararja Partap Singh and Raja Amar Singh to cater the needs of the public of this region. Its main objective was to promote the Dogra civilization, art and culture and its democratic and secular character including Hindus, Muslims and Dalits. It represented all communities of the State right from Kangra (H.P.), Hoshiarpur, Gurdaspur (Punjab), Mirpur, Poonch and other parts of Dogra terrain Daya Krishan Gardish, Vakil Hazat Shah, Mian Jawala Singh and Lala Hans Raj were the founder members of Dogra Sadar Sabha, Jammu.

Lala Hans Raj Mahajan, General Samunder Khan, Sardar Budh Singh, Sh. Jia Lai Kilam, Assad Uillah Shah Vakil, "*Jagat Ram Aryan (Harijan)*", Master Ram Rakha, Mulkh Raj Saraf, Col. Budhi Singh, Wazir Ganga Ram, Syed Mubarak Shah, Dewan N.D. Nargis, Sahibzada Hassan Shah, Pt. Ganesh Dass Shastri, Thakur Jawala Singh, Pt. Anant Ram, Col. Peer Mohammad, Sh. Mubarak Shah, Pt. Prem Nath Dogra, Sheikh Ali Mohd. Sodagar, Pt. Visheshwar Jyotishi etc. were the prominent personalities who played prominent and distinguished role in the service of the state under the banner of the Dogra Sadar Sabha. Moreover, this Sabha also had ladies wing which was incharged by Mrs. Mumtaz Begum.

Role of Separatist in Dogra Sadar Sabha = Latest Study of Huriyata Conference

At that time, Choudhary, Allah Rakha Sagar, Ch. Ghulam Abbas, Munshi Mehraj-ud-Din, Master Mohd. Akbar, Ch. Hamid Ullah etc, were the chief exponents of separatist ideology. But they also cooperated and supported the mission of the Dogra Sadar Sabha, Jammu.

Mission and objective of Dogra Sadar Sabha

The objective of this Sabha was to bring social and political reforms in the state. It was meant for the upliftment of the people of the state. Thus, it laid emphasis on the following issues:

1. To prohibit the juvenile delinquency, drinking and smoking.
2. To check the burial of female infants.
3. To check the drinking and dancing (*Mujras*) menace and other social and moral evils.
4. To check dowry, infant marriages and caste discrimination especially with *Harijans*.
5. To arrange the marriages of poor girls and help widows monetarily, with sewing machines and encouraging widow marriage.
6. To motivate public to take agriculture and farming.

7. To bring the burning problems to the notice of the authorities, especially provision of irrigation, drinking water, electricity facilities and arrangements of supply of food-grains during draught.

Inspite of above written objectives, Dogra Sadar Sabha had a great contribution in the state politics such as:

1. **Praja Parishad (Legislature Assembly):** It was a great contribution during the Maharaja's rule that it took initiative for the constitution of Praja Parishad (Legislative Assembly) and election of its members.
2. **State Subject Certificate:** The introduction of the state subject-certificate to safeguard the interests of the native inhabitants was also a great contribution of the Dogra Sadar Sabha.
3. **Freedom of Press:** Credit went to Dogra Sadar Sabha in the field of freedom of press. Freedom of press provided a platform to the people to raise their voice for their problems.
4. **Education:** It also provided free education and scholarship to the needy students and establishment of high schools and colleges.
5. **Constructioin of Chinab Bridge, at Akhnoor:** Dogra Sadar Singh also put great efforts for the construction of Chinab Bridge at Akhnoor for the smooth connectivity of people with the rest part of the region.
6. **Campaign Against Untouchability:** This Sabha had great vision of fraternity, communal harmony and peace. In order to remove disparity and social evils, it laucned a campaign against untouchability. This efforts brought the Dogra Sadar Sabha in the fore-front in the service of the public and it enjoyed full confidence of all the section of the society of this region.
7. **Supporter of Indian National Congress:** Dogra Sadar Sabha had provided its whole heartedly support to the Indian National Congress in the Indian National Movement. Thus, it was declared unconstitutional in 1929 A.D. and its activities remained banned for a few years.

   After independence, new social and political forces emerged in the state so Dogra Sadar Sabha remained inactive. It carried on usual social and other philanthropic works in the area.

   Due to discord in its organizational ranks, the Sabha remained under the administrative control of the then Dy. Commissioner,

Jammu, for the major portion of 1991,1992 and 1993 and due to the intervention of saner elements, the charge was restored to its workers in October 1993.

Revival of Dogra Sadar Sabha

Dogra Sadar Sabha was revived in 1993 with the common consensus of all sections of the society of this region.

Ideology of the Dogra Sadar Sabha

- Secular Values = Drug Addiction ke story.
- Democratic Values = Feedom struggle of the Dalit race.
- To safeguard the interests of the inhabitants of the soil at this critical juncture.

Mission of Dogra Sadar Sabha: This Sabha is reorgnised as Sabha units at grass-root level. Ladies and youth are to be fully associated and trained to discharge their active role in this respect. The following goals have been set as its mission-.

1. Equitable share in the developmental and progressive works in all the three regions of the state.
2. Equitable share in education, services and other government concerns.
3. Due representation in constituted and elected bodies.
4. Safeguard and promotion of "*Dogri language, Dogra civilization*" or "*Chamar Civilization*", art, culture, ancient heritage of monuments, historical buildings and ancient historical records found in the early history of Jammu Region. (Dr. Raj Kumar)
5. Safeguard and promotion of secular and democratic values due participation of representatives of all the three regions of the state in the negotiated settlement of Kashmir issue to ensure permanent peace, tranquility and well-being in this region.
6. To uphold the unity and integrity of the motherland.
7. To espouse the genuine demands of the public and work for the redressal of their grievances.

The following some important personalities of Dogra Sadar Sabha who honoured the chair as its presidents Idiot Brahmins = Rajput Community:

1. SadarBudh Singh 1904-1906
2. Jyotishi Pt. Vishveshwar 1906-1916

3. Sh.Avtar Singh 1964-1967
4. Sh. Dhian Singh 1969-1972
5. Vaid Vaishno Dutt 1972-1975
6. Sh. Mukund Lai Bharti 1976-1980
7. Dr. Gauri Shankar 1981-1981
8. Th. Gulchain Singh Charak 1990-till date

Presently, Th. Gulchain Singh Charak Pt. is president of the Dogra Sadar Sabha. K.P.Singh, Prem Singh Gupta, G.A. Khwaja, Brig. Rtd. M.S.Jamwal, S.Hakumat Singh, S.Kulbir Singh are the senior leaders of the Dogra Sadar Sabha. It has been demanding special recruitment drive in Police, Military and Para-Military forces from the border and Kandi belts of Jammu region. It has raised the issue of giving honour to Late Chamail Singh, who was murdered in Pakistani jail and to ensure compensation to the family at par with the family of Sarabjeet Singh of Punjab, who also killed under similar circumstances before the Government of India.

Note: Latest published work of the author "Encyclopeadia of Untouchables"; pp. 1-127 = History of the English literature + To close the chapter of Gandhian –Nehru Politics + Ajit Angral ke story as a principal = boot-polish culture against the school, college teachers = to pempure the political leaders that there is no authentic writer or ruler in this state = anti=Dalit propaganda. Dalit-English literature started by Lord Clive = Idea of New Christianity = there is no punishment, but due to the penetration of Brahmin-Rajputs in East Indian Company = there was anti-dalit literature. **Note:** Dalit literature begins with Chamar thought in India during the rule of Shahjahan. Study shows that was the era of infinite knowledge = in modern view, it is called globalisation of "**Indian History**" from pre-historic to Dr. D.K. Sury (Ibid).

Chapter - 6

Instrument of Accession= New Constitution of India = Dalit History of the State

Note: = *Comparative analysis used in History by the author.*

Historical Background

Jammu and Kashmir was a princely state. It was run by the Dogra Dynasty i.e. under the regime of Maharaja Gulab Singh, Maharaja Ranbir Singh. Maharaja Pratap Singh, and Maharaja Hari Singh. After the establishment of the National Conference and its New (Naya) Kashmir Manifesto. Maharaja Hari Singh of Jammu and Kashmir State brought reforms in His Administration by appointing two popular ministers in His cabinet—Mirza Afzal Beg, a nominee of National Conference and Wazir Ganga Ram.

Arrival of the Cabinet Mission

The Cabnet Mission arrived in India on 23rd March, 1946 to find a solution for the Indian problem and to review the relationship of the Indian Native Princes with the paramount power. Shiekh Mohammad Abdullah sent a letter to its for the same and made a request to re-examine this relationship. But the Cabinet Mission refused to consider the representation of the State's people. As a result, Mirza Afzal Beg resigned from the Maharaja's administration His resignation became the cause of His Highness to quit the State at that time society was based two groups Hindus and Muslims and Dalit were deprive section of the society.

Quit Kashmir Movement = 1942

Shiekh Mohammad Abdullah, the leader of the National Conference, challenged the Dogra sovereignty in Kashmir. He rejected the Treaty of

Amritsar between the British and Maharaja Gulab Singh; and started a movement against Maharaj Hari Singh to quit the Valley and leave the Kashmiris alone to decide their future by themselves. The movement was the Quit (India) Kashmir Movement in which he demanded for a Responsible Government.

The Maharaja's Government was prepared to meet such kind of situation. Thus, Sheikh Mohammad Abdullah was arrested and simply imprisoned for three years. His arrest and trial left a great impact on the public both in India and in Kashmir. India National Congress leaders, Pt. Jawahar Lal Nehru tried to visit Kashmir on 18th June 1947, but he was not allowed to enter the state by the Orders of the Maharaja. A Magistrate of the Maharaja's Government had informed Nehru about ban on his entry in Kashmir at Kohala. He advised him to go back to the British India. But Nehru turned a deaf ear to his advice. At Domel, Nehru was arrested and kept in detention for two days.

Role of the Muslim Conference

The Muslim Conference, another political organization in the valley, opposed the ideology of the National Conference and in July 1946, its president, Ghulam Abbas described the '*Quit Kashmir Movement*' as a '*Counsel of Despair*'. The Muslim Conference supported the actions of the Maharaja's Government and continued to participate in the legislative proceedings till September, 1946. Meanwhile, the Muslim Conference in Kashmir began advocating the Muslim League's Cause in Kashmir. Ghulam Abbas appealed to the Maharaja to release Sheikh Abdullah. The Maharaja realized the danger from Abbas group also. Hence, Ghulam abbas and other prominent leaders of the Muslim Conference were arrested for the '*Security of the state.*'

Memorandum of the Cabinet Mission Plan

On 25th may, 1946, the Cabinet Mission issued the Memorandum dated May 12,1946, in regard to State's treaties and Paramountcy. In this memorandum, the Mission affirmed that the rights of the states which flowed from their relationship with the Crown would no longer exist and the rights surrendered by the States to the Paramount Power would revert to the states when the Two New Dominions of India and Pakistan are created. (For more details se "*appendix 4*"). In other words, it reflected the shift of power from the British to the newly emerging states of India and Pakistan. (Study the book *"Last Years of the British Rule in India"*)

Lord Mountbatten's Address to the Chamber of Princes as Christians Pt.

On 25th July, 1947, Lord Mountbatten addressed the Chamber of Princes and advised the Princes and their representatives to accede to one or other of the Dominions before the Transfer of Power, keeping in mind the geographical contact of their states'. He threw light on the meaning of the accession. Under the Cabinet Mission Memorandum of 1947, accession meant to surrender of only three subjects Defence, External Affairs and communications to the Central Government. He advised them to join either of the Dominion; otherwise they might be cut off from any source of supply. For it, he circulated the copies of a draft Instrument of Accession for discussion. A state could accede to either Dominion by Executing an Instrument of Accession signed by the Ruler and accepted by the Governor-General of the Dominion concerned.

Standstill Agreement of the Maharaja

Most of the leaders of the National Conference and Muslim League were in prison during the time of Independence of India. The people of state again started their demand for Responsible Government. In the ansence of the British help, Maharaja Hari Singh found himself in a tight corner. He opted for the standstill agreement with both India and Pakistan. He sent two identical telegrams to both nations. After independence, Pakistan pressurized the Maharaja to join Pakistan.

The Poonch Revolt

Meanwhile, in the second week of August, the *'Poonch Revolt'* against the authority of Maharaja occurred. This revolt was due to infiltration from Pakistan. Pakistan continued to pressurize the Maharaja to accede and started creating tensions in the region by economic blockade, cutting the supply of essential commodities, military pressure by hit and run border raids, etc. Even the people of Kashmir were not ready to bow before imperialist and colonial designs of Pakistan.

Release of Sheikh Mohammad Abdullah

On the advice of his Prime-Minister (Pt. Jawahar Lal Nehru), Maharaja released Shiekh Mohammad Abdullah on 29th September, 1947. Sheikh Abdullah addressed a public meeting in Srinagar where he repeated the main demand of the Kashmiris as 'Freedom before Accession'. (Further details see Appendix 5)

Tribal Invasion = Adavasi Culture

Jinnah became impatient. In the state of frustration and confusion, he directed the tribesmen to invade Kashmir. On 20th October 1947, a number of tribesmen armed with 'bren guns, machine guns, mortars and flame throwers attacked the frontier of the state. Srinagar trembled before the danger of this invasion. It brought great destruction to Kashmir. The Maharaja as very upset because the Dogra Army and the National Militia (a volunteer Militia force formed by the National Conference) were unable to hold the tribal attack called as Sindhi Culture.

Approach to the Indian Government for Military Assistance

The tribal invasion compelled the Maharaja Hari Singh to approach the Government of India for immediate military assistance. On the other hand, the Indian leadership showed its helplessness (compulsion) before the establishment of popular government in Kashmir and without signing of the Instrument of Accession of the State to the Indian Government.(Study the book of the author; *Maharaja Gulab Singh & His Race)*

Sheikh Abdullah's Advice to Maharaja for the Safety of the State

At the time of crisis, Sheikh Mohammad Abdullah advised the Maharaja, about the safety of the State, to accede to India and ask for immediately military assistance. Maharaja Hari Singh accepted it and appointed him as the Emergency Administrator and left Srinagar on 25th October 1947 to save his life and went to Jammu— the winter capital of the State.

Letter to Lord Mountbatten alongwith the Instrument of Accession Duly signed by the Maharaja Hari Singh

Maharja Hari Singh wrote a letter on 26th October to Lord Mountbatten - 'the Governor-General of Free India in which he explained about the cirisis in the valley, the tribal invasion etc. (for further details, see appendix 6). The copy of Instrument of Accession of Jammu and Kashmir was also attached.

Instrument of Accession of Jammu and Kashmir State = Brahminonat

Whereas, the Independence Act, 1947, provides that as from the fifteenth day of August, 1947, there shall be setup an independent Dominion known as INDIA, and that the government of India Act, 1935, shall with such omissions, additions, adaptations, and modifications as the Governor-General may by order specify, be applicable to the Dominion of India;

And whereas the Government of India Act, 1935, as so adapted by the governor-General provides that an Indian State may accede to the Dominion of India by an Instrument of Accesion executed by the Ruler thereof;

Now, therefore, I Shriman Indar Mahandar Rajrajeshwar Maharajadhiraj Shri Hari Singh ji Jammu Kashmir Naresh Tatha Tibbetadi Deshadhipathi Ruler of ***Jammu and Kashmir*** State in the exercise of my sovereignty in and over my said state do hereby execute this my Instrument of Accession and —

1. I hereby declare that I accede to the Dominion of India with the intent that the Governor-General of India, the Dominion Legislature, the Federal Court and any other Dominion authority established for the purposes of the Dominion shall, by virtue of this my Instrument of Accession, but subject always to the terms thereof, and for the purposes of the Dominion, exercise in relation to the state of Jammu and Kashmir (hereinafter referred to as "this state") such functions as may be vested in them by or under the Government of India Act, 1935, as in force in the Dominions of India on the 15th August, 1947 (which Act as so in force is hereinafter referred to as "the Act".)
2. I hereby assume the obligation of ensuring that due effect is given to the provisions of the Act within this State so far as they are applicable therein by virtue of this my Instrument of Accession.
3. I accept the matters specified in the Schedule hereto as the matters with respect to which the Dominion Legislature may make laws for this State.
4. I hereby declare that I accede to the Dominion of India on the assurance that if an agreement is made between the Governor-General and the Ruler of this State. Whereby any functions in relation to the administration in this State of any law of the Dominion Legislature shall be exercised by the ruler of this State, then any such agreement shall be deemed to form part of this Instrument and shall be construed and have effect accordingly.
5. The terms of this my Instrument of Accession shall not be variedly any amendment of the Act or of the Indian Independence Act, 1947, unless such amendment is accepted by an Instrument supplementary to this Instrument.

6. Nothing in this Instrument shall empower the Dominion Legislature to make any law for this State authorizing the compulsory acquisition of land for any purpose, but I hereby undertake that should the Dominion for the purpose of a Dominion Law which applies in this State deem it necessary to acquire my land, I will at their requisite acquire the land at their expense or if the land belongs to me transfer it to them on such terms as may be agreed, or in default of agreement, determined by an arbitrator to be appointed by the Chief Justice of India from Raja to Praja or the rule of the common people.
7. Nothing in this Instrument shall be deemed to commit me in any way to acceptance of any future Constitution of India or to fetter my discretion to enter into arrangements with the Government of India under any such future constitution.
8. Nothing in this Instrument affects the Continuance of my sovereignty in and over this state, or save as provided by or under this Instrument, the exercise or any powers, authority and rights now enjoyed by me as Ruler of this State or the validity of any law at present in force in this State.
9. Thereby declare that I execute this Instrument on behalf of this State and that any reference in this Instrument to me or to the Ruler of the State is to be construed as including a reference of my heirs and successors.

Given under my hand this 26th day of October Nineteen Hundred and Forty-Seven

(Sd.) HARI SINGH
Maharaj adhiraj of Jammu and Kashmir state.)

I do hereby accept this Instrument of Accession.

Dated this Twenty-Seventh day of October Nineteen Hundred and Forty-Seven.

(Sd/-) MOUNTBATTEN of BURMA
(Governor-General of India)

Note:- The "*History of the Dalit Parivar*", it begins with the idelogy of Dr. B.R. Ambedkar called as Chandal or Mahar in South India, and Brahmin like Maharaja Hari Singh had dominated the Dalit concept as a new discovery of the human race called as "Western Ideology". (Dr. D.K. Surya)

Chapter - 7

Special Status, Article 370 of the Indian Constitution and Presidential Order of 1954 = Old Chapter of "Kashmir Issue"

Note: = *Comparative analysis used in History by the author.*

With the accession of the state of Jammu and Kashmir to India, jurisdiction in matters of External Affairs, Defence and Communication was transferred to the Government of India and the Union Parliament was given power to make laws for the State for the purposes of those three matters only. Sovereignty still remained with the ruler so far as the internal administration of the State was concerned. The state was governed by the Jammu and Kashmir Constitution Act, 1939. Under this Act, Maharaja Hari Singh appointed Shiekh Mohammad Abdullah in 1947, the Emergency Administrator for the State. But people demanded Responsible Government and framing of their own Constitution. Maharaja appointed Yuvraj Karan Singh as ruler of the state on 20th June 1949 and left the state for Bombay as a member of the Nehru -Gandhi family and died in 1960. One Brahmin Concept.

The Constitution of India came into force on 26th January, 1950 alongwith Article 370. Sardar Patel, the then Minister for States in India, declared in the Indian Constituent Assembly, "in view of the special problem with which the Jammu and Kashmir is faced, we have made special provisions for the continuance of the State with the Union on the existing basis."(See Plate-I Dr B.R. Ambedkar and his fellow – friends Sardar Patel and Nehru, Mulana Azad, etc.)

The existing basis' were the basis of Instrument of Accession and the Special Provisions were embodies in Article 370 of the constitution of India, which reads as follows:-

Temporary Provisions with respect to the State of Jammu and Kashmir

"1. Notwithstanding anything in this Constitution-

(a) The provision of article 238 shall not apply in relation to the State of Jammu and Kashmir.

(b) The power of the Parliament to make laws for the said State shall be limited to;

(i) Those matters in the Union List and the Concurrent List which, in consultation with the Government of State, are declared by the President to correspond to matters specified in the Instrument of Accession governing the Accession of the State to the Dominion of India as the matters with respect to which the Dominion Legislature may make laws for that State; and

(ii) Such other matters in the aid list as, with the concurrence of the Government of the State, the President may be order specify.

(c) The provisions of article 1 and of this article shall apply in relation to that State;

(d) Such of the other provisions of this constitution shall apply in relation to that State subject to such exceptions and modifications as the President may by order specify:

(e) Provided further that no such order which relates to the matters other than those referred to in the last preceding provision shall be issued except with the concurrence of that Government.

2. If the concurrence of the Government of the State referred to in paragraph (ii) of sub-clause (b) of clause (1) or in the second provision to sub-clause (d) of the clause be given before the Constituent Assembly for the purpose of framing the Constitution-of the State is convened, it shall be placed before such Assembly for such decision as it may take thereon.

3. Notwithstanding anything in the foregoing provisions of this article the President may, by public notification, declare that this Article shall cease to be operative or shall be operative only with' such exceptions and modifications and from such date as he may specify:

Provided that the recommendation of the Constituent Assembly referred to in clause (2) shall be necessary before the President issues such a notification."

Sardar Patel explained this Article 370 as a device to continue the existing relationship of the Jammu and Kashmir state with the Union of India upto the strong state of India (2017).

Main Provisions of Article 370 in the Part 21 of the Indian Constitution

The following are the main provisions of this article which are only temporary and not permanent and became operative on 17th November 1952:—

1. The provision of Article 1 (declaring India as a Union of States and its territory) and this article 370 are applicable to the state of Jammu and Kashmir for the strengthen of forces.
2. The provisions of Article 23 8 of the Indian Constitution are not applicable to this state.
3. Article 370 is a special provision for amending the constitution in its applicable to the Jammu and Kashmir State. Article 368 does not curtail the power of the President under Article 370.
4. It refers (clause (l)(b) of the Article 370) to the legislature authority of Parliament over Jammu and Kashmir State. The Union parliament had power to make laws for the state over those matters which were covered in the Instrument of Accession i.e. Defence, External Affairs, Communication."
5. Others items of list 1 should be settled by agreement between the President and the Kashmir Government.
6. The Constitution of India clearly considered the convening of a Constituent Assembly for Jammu and Kashmir State.
7. Article 246 has been applied only with some modifications of the State of Jammu and Kashmir. As a result, the State Legislature of Jammu and Kashmir has a residuary power of legislation over matters which may not be enumerated in the State List or the Concurrent List.

Presidential Order of 1954

The Presidential Order of 1954, also known as the Constitution Order Application to Jammu and Kashmir, 1954 deals only with the Constitutional position of the State of Jammu and Kashmir within the framework of the Indian Constitution. This order of 1954 superseded the earlier order of 1950 and extended the Union's jurisdiction over the State. This is the basic order that regulates the constitutional position of the

State and its relationship with the Union. The following are the important provisions of this order:—

1. Jammu and Kashmir is a constituent State of the Indian union and has its place in Part I and Schedule 1 of the Indian Constitution.
2. The name, area or boundary of the State cannot be changed by the Union without the consent of its legislature.
3. The state of Jammu and Kashmir has its own Constitution and is administered according to that Constitution.
4. The provisions of Part II regarding the denial of citizenship rights of migrants to Pakistan are not applicable to the permanent residents of Jammu and Kashmir, who after having so migrated to Pakistan return to the state for resettlement.
5. Part III dealing with Fundamental Rights is applicable to the State with some exceptions and conditions. The Fundamental Right to Property is guaranteed in the state.
6. Certain special rights are granted to the permanent residents of the state with regard to public employment, acquisition of immovable property, settlement and government scholarships.
7. Part IV dealing with the Directive Principles of State Policy and Part IV, a dealing with Fundamental Duties are not applicable to the State (Dalits).
8. Parliament can make laws in relations to the state on most of the subjects enumerated in the Union List and on a good number of subjects enumerated in the Concurrent List.
9. A National emergency declared on the ground of internal disturbance will not have effect in the state except with the concurrence of the state government.
10. The President has no power to declare a financial emergency in relation to the State.
11. The President has no power to suspend the State Constitution on the ground of failure to comply with the directions given by him.
12. The State Emergency (President's Rule) is applicable to the State. However, this emergency can be imposed in the state or the ground of failure of the Constitutional Machinery under the provisions of State Constitution and not Indian Constitution. In fact, two types of Emergencies can be declared in the State namely President's Rule under the Indian Constitution and Governor's rule under the State Constitution.

13. An Amendment made to the Constitution of India does not apply to the state unless it is extended by a Presidential Order.
14. The fifth schedule and the sixth schedule are not applicable to the state.
15. The special leave jurisdiction of the Supreme Court and the jurisdictions of the Election Commission and the Comptroller and Auditor General are applicable to the State;.
16. The High Court of Jammu and Kashmir can issue writs only for the enforcement of the fundamental rights and not for any other purpose.

Note:- In this chapter we deal with the '*Gilgit Agency*' as forward Choki of the natural boundry of India territory (1877-1935) at the rate of Gmail.com as an appointment of Dalit historiam like Maharaja Suchet Singh now called Prof. Suteel Ved. (A.S. Chohan; *The Gilgit Agency*; Preface)

Chapter - 8

Permanent Residents of Jammu and Kashmir and their Rights = Dalit Literature

I

Historical Background: Before Independence, Maharaja Gulab Singh, Ranbir Singh and Partap Singh

The people of Jammu And Kashmir State had agitated for the protection of their rights against the superior competing interests of the non-residents of the state. During the regime of Maharaja Pratap Singh, a number of educated persons from outside the state were brought and recruited in the state services because of non-availability of educated people in the State. It was in response to this popular agitation that the Maharaja's Government issued a Notification No. 1-L 84 dated 20th of April, 1927 providing the definition of the term "State-Subject" as sanctioned by the Maharaja vide Private Secretary's Letter No, 2354, dated 31st of January, 1927. This Notification was followed by Notification No. 13-L dated 27th of June, 1932 under the command of the Maharaja for the purposes of determining the status of the State-Subjects in foreign countries and to inform the concerned Government's as to the position of their nationalism in the State of Jammu and Kashmir as a new concept of the Dalit State.

II

Historical Background: After Independence

The Constitution of Indian came into force on 26th January, 1950 having the Article 370 special status for Jammu and Kashmir State. In 1954, the Constituent Assembly of Jammu and Kashmir ratified the State's accession to India and set a controversy regarding the future affiliations of the state at rest. Here, a great discussion began between the representatives of India and Kashmir about the "*Separate Citizenship of the State*". After a long discussion, the matter was settled that the Permanent Residents of Jammu and Kashmir State could have special rights but they were to have the common Indian citizenship. It was agreed that the term 'State Subjects' be deleted and in its place Permanent Residents' be substituted for such persons who were State subjects under the provisions of the state subjects Notification of 1927.

In consultation with the State Government, the President of India issued the Constitutional Order (Application to Jammu and Kashmir), 1954 which included the essentials for the Permanent Residents of the state. Later, on, these are included in the Part III entitled 'Permanent Residents' Section 6 to 10 in the Constitution of Jammu and Kashmir:-

III

Permanent Resident Dalit History.

Section 6 Permanent Residents—

(1) Every person who is, or is deemed to be, a citizen of India under the provisions of the Constitution of India shall be a permanent resident of the State, if on the 14th Day of May, 1954:—
   (a) he was a state Subject of Class I or the Class II; or
   (b) having lawfully acquired immovable property in the state, he has been ordinarily resident in the state for not less than ten years prior to the date.

(2) any person who, before the fourteen day of May, 1954, was a state subject of Class I or of class II and who having migrated after the first day of March, 1947, to the territory now included in Pakistan returns to the State under a permit of resettlement in the State or for permanent return issued by or under the authority of any law made by the State Legislature shall on such return be a permanent resident of the State.

Section 7. Constitution of References to State Subjects in Existing Laws

Unless the context otherwise requires all references in any existing law of hereditary State Subjects or to State Subjects of class I or of Class II or of Class III shall be construed as references to permanent residents of the state.

Section 8. Legislature to Define Permanent Residents

Nothing in the forging provision of this part shall derogate from the power of the State Legislature to make any law defining the classes of persons who are, or shall be, permanent residents of the state.

Section 9. Special Provision for Bill Relating to Permanent Residents

A Bill making provision for any of the following matters, namely: -

(a) Defining or altering the definition of the classes of persons who are or shall be, permanent residents of the state;

(b) Conferring on permanent residents any special rights or privileges;

(c) Regulating or modifying any special rights or privileges enjoyed by permanent residents, shall be deemed to be passed by either House of the Legislature only if it is passed by a majority of not less than two-thirds of the total membership of that House.

Section 10. Rights of the Permanent Residents

The Permanent Residents of the state shall have all the rights guaranteed to them under the constitution of India

Thus, on the basis of Section 10 of the Constitution of Jammu and Kashmir, the Permanent Resident of Jammu and Kashmir are enjoying all Fundament Rights as guaranteed by the Constitution of India.

Note:- Politics of Kashmir is a propaganda of Dalit historian late strong Brahmin of Kashmir called Kashyap Rishi (1500 B.C. and so on).

These follow as under:-

Fundamental Rights of the Citizens and Advancement knowledge of Dalit Family of Kashmir.

Part III of the Indian Constitution deals with the fundamental rights. These rights are written in the constitution. These have been described as Indian Magna Carta of rights and freedoms. These are enforceable in nature. The following are the six fundamental rights of the Indian citizens:

1. Right to Equality (Articles 14-18)
2. Right to Freedom (Articles 19-22)
3. Right against exploitation (Articles 23-24)
4. Right to Freedom of Religion(Articles 25-28)

5. Cultural and Educational Rights (Articles 29-30)
6. Right to Constitutional Remedies (Articles 32)

Note: Right to property has been deleted from the list of Fundamental Rights by the 44th Amendment and made a legal right under Article 300-A

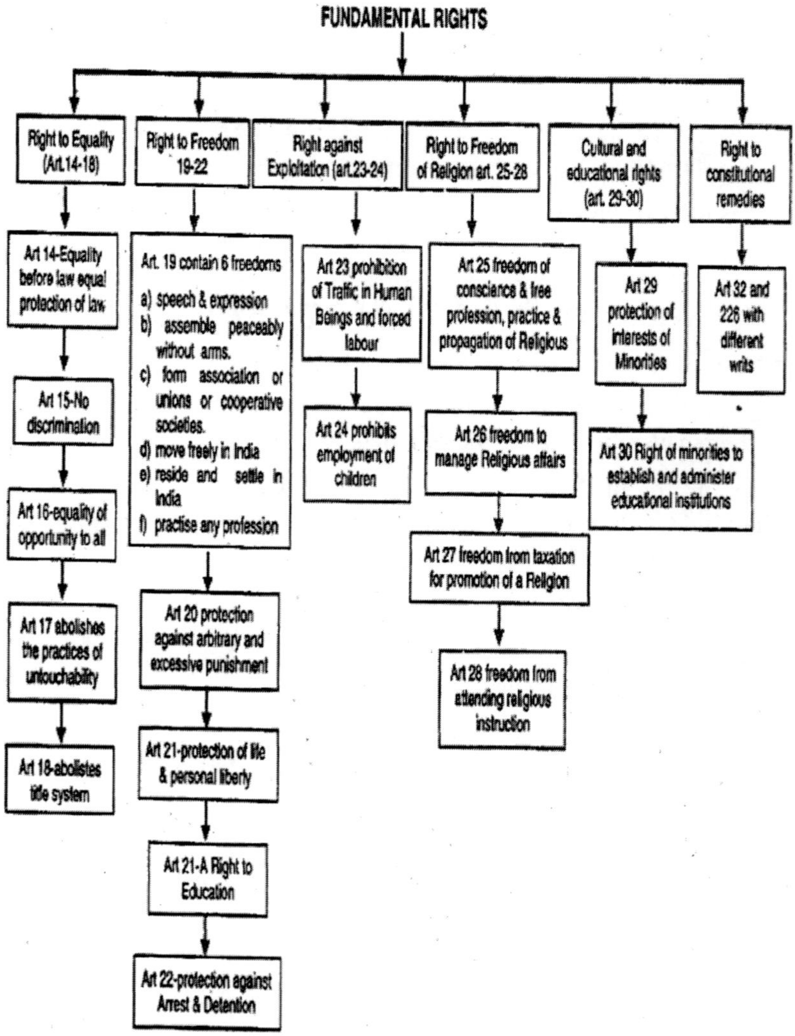

1. **Right to Equality (Articles 14-18):**
   (a) Article 14 states that the state shall not deny to any person equality before law and equal protection of the laws within the territory of India.
   (b) Article 15 provides that the state shall not discriminate against any citizen on grounds only of religion, race, caste, sex or place or birth.,
   (c) Article 16 provides for equality of opportunity for all citizens in the matters of employment or appointment to any office under the state. It further states that no citizen shall on grounds of religion, race, caste, sex, descent place of birth, residence or any of them be discriminated against in respect of any employment or office under the state.
   (d) Article 17 abolishes the evil practice of untouchability in India. Its practice in any form, considers an offence punishable under the law.
   (e) Article 18: The constitution prohibits the state from conferring any titles except honours for military and academic distinctions.

2. **Right to Freedom (Articles 19-22):**
   (a) **Article 19**: Article 19 of the Indian Constitution grants six rights to its citizens:
      (i) Right to freedom of speech and expression.
      (ii) Right to assemble peaceably and without arms.
      (iii) Right to form association or union or co-operative societies (The provision for "Co-operative Societies" is made by the 97th Constitutional Amendment Act of 2011)
      (iv) Right to move freely throughout the territory of India.
      (v) Right to reside and settle in any part of the territory of India.
      (vi) Right to practise any profession to carry on any occupation, trade or business.
   (b) **Article 20**: Article 20 grants protection against arbitrary and excessive punishment to an accused person, whether citizen or foreigner or legal person like a company or a corporation. It contains three provisions in that direction.
      (i) **No Export Facto Law:** No person shall be convicted of any offence except for violation of a law in force at the time of the commission of the act.; nor subjected to an penally greater

than that prescribed by the law in force at the time of the commission of the act.

(ii) **No double Teopardy:** No person shall be prosecuted and punished for the same offence more than once.

(iii) **No-self Incrimination:** No person accused of any offence shall be compelled to be a witness against himself.

(c) **Article 21** declares that no person shall be deprived of his life or personal liberty except according to procedure established by law. This right is available to both citizens and non-citizens = Natural Dandniti to control the anti-Dalit propaganda.

(d) **Article 21** A declares that the state shall provide free and compulsory education to all children of the age of six to fourteen years in such a manner as the state may determine.

(Note: This Article 21A is added by the 86th Constitutional Amendment Act. of 2002. It makes only the elementary education as a Fundamental Right.)

(e) **Article 22** grants protection to persons against arbitrary arrest and detention. It lays down that a person who is arrested and detained shall be:

(i) Informed of the ground of his arrest and shall have the right to consult and be defended by a legal practitioner of his choice.

(ii) produced before the nearest magistrate within a period of 24 hours of his arrest excluding the time taken in journey from the place of his arrest to the court of the magistrate. He cannot be detained in custody beyond 24 hours without the authority of the Magistrate.

3. Right Against Exploitation (Articles 23-24):

(a) **Article 23** prohibits traffic in human beings, beggar (forced labour) and other similar form of forced labour. The traffic in human beings includes (i) selling and buying of men, women and children like goods; immoral traffic in women and children including prostitution, devadasis, slavery, etc.

(b) **Article 24** prohibits the employment of children below the age of 14 years in any factory, mine or other hazardous activities like construction work or railway.

4. Rights of Freedom of Religion (Articles 25-28):

(a) **Article 25** grants to all persons, the freedom of conscience and the right to profess, practise and propagate any religion.

(b) **Article 26** states that every religious denomination or any of its section shall have the following rights:

 (i) to establish and maintain institution for religious and charitable purposes;

 (ii) to manage its own affairs in matters of religion;

 (iii) to own and acquire movable and immovable property; and

 (iv) to administer such property in accordance with law.

(c) **Article 27** lays down that no person shall be compelled to pay any taxes for the promotion or maintenance of any particular religion or religious denomination.

(d) Under Article 28, no religious instruction shall be provided in any educational institution wholly maintained out of state funds or receiving aid from the state.

5. Cultural and Educational Rights (Articles 29-30):

(a) **Article 29** provides that any section of the citizen residing in any part of India having a distinct language, script or culture of its own, shall have the right to conserve the same.

(b) Under Article 30, the state grants all minorities shall have the right to establish and administer educational institutions of their choice.

6. Right to Constitutional Remedies (Article 32)

Right to Constitutional Remedies makes the fundamental rights meaningful because if any person violates the rights of others, then they have the right to remedies for the enforcement of the fundamental rights. In other words, it means that fundamental rights are also protected through this fundamental right itself.

The Supreme Court rules that Article 32 is a basic feature of the constitution. The Supreme Court and High Courts have the power to issue directions or orders or writs for the enforcement of any of the fundamental rights. The writ jurisdiction ensures that the courts can protect the citizens from those who hold public power in their hands.

The monarch of England used to exercise certain prerogative writs to review the actions taken by the officer under the monarch's seal. If any subject of the monarch had any problem with any action taken by the officials of the monarchy, being the highest political authority, king was the only one who could review those actions (Nam). Later on, all those societies which emerged as constitutional democracies, the sovereignty got vested in the people and its manifestation emerged in the form of political document called "the Constitution". So all those actions of the public officials are now reviewed by the courts of law in their capacity as the guardians of the Constitution of a country. The following are five major prerogative writs exercised by the Supreme Court and the High Court under Articles 32 and 226 respectively so whenever the fundamental rights of any citizen of the country and non-citizen are threatened by action of the public authority, the writ jurisdiction of the constitutional courts can be invoked:

1. Habeas Corpus: The writ of Habeas Corpus is one of the most ancient writs known in the English judicial system and to all those legal systems modelled on the English judicial system. The Latin Phrase '*Habeas Corpus*' means '*have the body*' of God and Man. This writ protects a person from any illegal detention and through this writ, the court directs the person or authority who has detained another person to bring the body of the prisoner before the court so that the court may decide the validity and justification of such detention. This writ provides a prompt and effective remedy against illegal restraints. For example; someone is forcibly detained by a police officer or someone has already undergone a detention period but is not released, the aggrieved person or someone on his behalf can approach the court and can secure his or her release.

RIGHT TO CONSTITUTIONAL REMEDIES
(Art. 32 and 226)
Various writs

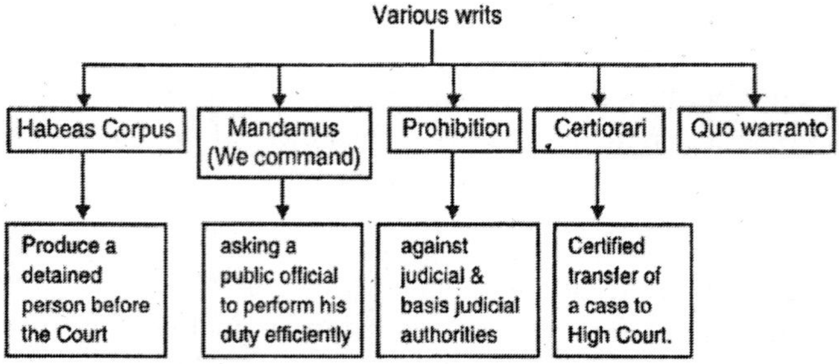

2. Mandamus: It means a command. It is an order issued by a court to a public authority asking it to perform a public duty imposed upon it by the constitution or by any other law. It is in the form of an order from a superior court to any government, court, corporation or public authority to do some specific action which that body is obliged under law to do good work under the leadership of Dr. B.R. Ambedkar as silence observer of the state. This remedy is available only in those cases where a public authority is under a legal duty to perform certain acts. The duty must be statutory i.e. either imposed by any specific law or by the constitution itself. This writ is general allowed only when there is a demand to the public authority and there is a refusal from that authority. So if . lets say a municipality if not maintain the drainage system many particular locality, or the concerned authority does not care to repair the uncovered and hanging electricity wires threatening the lives of the people of the area, the aggrieved persons can approach the court to get the administrative machinery moving.

3. Certiorari: The literal meaning of the term means "*to be certified*" or "*to be informed.*" It is issued by a superior court to any authority exercising public power requiring the records of any action which impacts the rights of an individual to be certified by the court and dealt with according to the law. In all those cases where the actions of the public power are constitutionally or legally untenable, the decisions of the public authority are declared null and void. So assume a particular tax authority imposes some tax on you and the authority does not have the power to impose such tax, you can get the decision declared null and void through the writ of certiori. Or assume a person is wrong removed from his job, the writ of certiorari can again be relied upon by the person to get the decision of removal tested by the court as equality base knowledge.

4. Prohibition: The writ of prohibition is very similar to the writ of *certiorari* in its elements. The only major difference between the two is the point of time when one is issued. The writ of prohibits is issued when the action of the public authority is still underway. In local parlance we also call it as the *'stay order'*. It basically establishes the status quo till the court pronounces upon the validity of the action of the public authority. Thus, this remedy prevents the public authorities from continuing their proceedings in excess or abuse of their jurisdiction or in violation of the principles of natural justice or in contravention of the law of the land, for example, if some people are forcibly evicted from any premises or some shops are to be demolished by government order, the aggrieved people can file for the writ of prohibition.

5. Quo Warranto: It means "by what warrant or authority." Through this remedy the court of a law requires a person occupying a public office to show by what right he claims it, so that the title of the office may be settled and any unauthorized or ineligible person is ousted. It is a method of judicial control in the sense that the proceedings practically review the actions of the administrative authority which appointed the person. This remedy has two aspects. On one side, this makes the administration more efficient by removing inefficient and unqualified personnel and imposters from public offices. On the other side, it protects a citizen from being deprived of a public office to which he has a right e.g. assume the appointment to a public office is done without the public notification and without giving equal opportunity to all those who were sufficiently qualified, such appointment can be challenged by the one who was denied the opportunity to compete.

Note:- The History of the Dalit Samaj as a new discovery begins with the ideology of Kanshi Ram and Ex.CM Mayawati in U.P. State etc. Now, the present Government Aditya Kumar Yogi, it is based on incomplete concept as modern Brahmins (Monkey- mind CM) of .U.P. Amit Shah is the founder of that state as a big snake of the world in human form, according the statement of Guru Nanak, presently called Dr. S.P. Gargotra R/o Nazla Chack, a poor peasant.

Chapter - 9

Constitution of Jammu and Kashmir as Especial Status for Dalits (Jammu)

The idea of framing a Constituent Assembly for Jammu and Kashmir State was imagined before the partition of India. After the Instrument of Accession, the Constituent Assembly was formed in 1951 for the establishment of the responsible democratic government in the state. It took about five years to complete its task. There were 12 sessions held from 29th September 1956 to 19th November, 1956. The Drafting Committee presented the draft constitution on 10th October 1956. After several long discussions, the constitution was approved and adopted on 17th November, 1956. The constitution of Jammu and Kashmir came into existence on 26th January 1957 alongwith its preamble.

The Preamble to the Constitution of Jammu and Kashmir Reads:

"We, the people of the State of Jammu and Kashmir, having solemnly resolved, in the presence of the accession of this state of India which took place on the twenty-sixth day of October, 1947", to further define the existing relationship of the state with the Union of India as an integral part thereof, and to secure to ourselves :-

JUSTICE, social, economic and political;

LIBERTY, of thought, expression, belief, faith and worship;

EQUALITY of status and of opportunity, and to promote among us all;

FRATERNITY assuring the dignity of the individual and the Unity of the Nation;

IN OUR CONSTITUENT ASSEMBLY this Seventeenth day of November, 1956, do hereby *ADOPT, ENACT AND GIVE TO OURSELVES THIS CONSTITUTION.*

The following are the important features of the constitution of Jammu and Kashmir:-

1. **Written Constitution:** Jammu and Kashmir State has a written Constitution. This document has 158 sections and schedules.
2. **Partly Rigid and Partly Flexible:** The Constitution of Jammu and Kashmir is partly rigid and partly flexible. The provision to section 147 specifies the rigid features of the constitution.
3. **Integral Part of India:** The Constitution of Jammu and Kashmir declares the state to be an integral part of India (Section 3 of the J&K Constitution)
4. **Territory of the State:** the territory of the state shall comprise all the territories which on the 15th August, 1947, were under the sovereignty or suzerainty of the ruler of the state (Section 4). This means that the territory of the ***state*** also includes the area which is under the enemy occupation of Pakistan.
5. **Justice, Liberty, Equality and Fraternity:** It secures justice, liberty, equality and fraternity to the people of the State.
6. **Parliamentary Form of Government:** The State Constitution establishes the parliamentary form of government in the State. The Head of the State (Governor) is a nominal head whereas the Chief-Minister is the real head of the State. The Council of Ministers are responsible for the Legislature.
7. **Permanent Residents of the State Nam or Kalma:** It lays down that a citizens of India is treated as a 'permanent resident of the state if on 14th May, 1954
   (a) He was a state subject of Class I or Class II or
   (b) Having lawfully acquired immovable property in the state, he has been ordinarily resident in the state for 10 years prior to that date or Temporary Provisions with respect to the State of Jammu and Kashmir.

   "1. Notwithstanding anything in this Constitution-
   (a) The provision of article 23 8 shall not apply in relation to the State of Jammu and Kashmir.
   (b) The power of the Parliament to make laws for the said State shall be limited to;
      (i) Those matters in the Union List and the Concurrent List which, in consultation with the Government of State, are declared by the President to correspond to matters

specified in the Instrument of Accession governing the Accession of the State to the Dominion of India as the matters with respect to which the Dominion Legislature may make laws for that State; and

(ii) Such other matters in the aid list as, with the concurrence of the Government of the State, the President may be order specify.

(c) The provisions of article 1 and of this article shall apply in relation to that State;

(d) Such of the other provisions of this constitution shall apply in relation to that State subject to such exceptions and modifications as the President may by order specify:

(e) Provided further that no such order which relates to the matters other than those referred to in the last preceding provision shall be issued except with the concurrence of that Government.

2. If the concurrence of the Government of the State referred to in paragraph (ii) of sub-clause (b) of clause (1) or in the second provision to sub-clause (d) of the clause be given before the Constituent Assembly for the purpose of framing the Constitution of the State is convened, it shall be placed before such Assembly for such decision as it may take thereon. (c) Any person who before 14th May, 1954 was a state subject of Class I or class II and who having migrated to Pakistan after 1st March 1947, returns to the state for resettlement.

8. **Fundamental Rights:** It states that the permanent residents of the state are entitled to all rights guaranteed under the Constitution of India. It does not contain a separate chapter on the fundamental rights. These rights are enforceable by any court.

9. **Directive Principles of the State Policy:** Part IV and Section 11 to 25 contain a list of Directive Principles of the State Policy. These principles are treated as fundamental in the governance of the state. It shall be the duty of the state to apply these principles in making laws. But they are not enforceable by any court.

10. **Bicameral Legislature:** Jammu and Kashmir State has bicameral legislature. It consists of two houses namely State Legislative Council as Upper House as State Legislative Assembly as Lower House.

The State Legislative Council consists of 36 members, most of them are elected in an indirect manner and eight of them are nominated by the Governor, who is also an integral part of the State Legislature.

The State Legislative Assembly consists of 111 members directly elected by the people. Out of this, 24 seats are to remain vacant as they are allotted for the area i.e. under the occupation of Pakistan. Thus, for the practical purposes, the total strength of the Assembly is to be taken as 87.

11. **Failure of the Constitutional Machinery in the State:** Under Section 92 of the State Constitutional machinery, if at any time, the governor is satisfied that a situation has arisen in which the Government of the state cannot be carried on in accordance with the provision of this constitution. The Governor can with the consent of the President issue a proclamation assuring the executive and legislative functions of the state.
12. **Governor's Rule:** It provides for Governor's Rule. The Governor, with the concurrence of the President of India, can assume to himself all the powers of the State Government, except those of the high court. He can dissolve the assembly and dismiss the council of ministers. The Governor's Rule can be imposed when the state administration cannot be carried on in accordance with the provisions of the Jammu and Kashmir Constitution.
13. **High Court:** It establishes a high court consisting of a chief Justice and two or more other judges. They are appointed by the President of India in consultation with the Chief Justice of India and the Governor of the State. The High court of Jammu and Kashmir is a Court of Record and enjoys original, appellate and writ jurisdictions.
14. **Executive Powers:** This Constitution provides the executive powers of the state in the Governor appointed by the President for a period of five years. It consists of a council of ministers headed by the Chief-Minister to aid and advise the Governor in the exercise of his functions. The Council of Ministers is collectively responsible to the Assembly.
15. **Periodic Election System:** Under section 138, Part X of the state constitution deals with the superintendence, direction and control of the preparation of the electoral rolls for and the conduct of elections to either House of the State Legislature.

16. **Universal Adult Suffrage:** Permanent resident of the state, who has completed the age of 18 years, has the right to vote.
17. **Tenure of the Government:** The state Government enjoys the tenure of **6** years to run the state.
18. **Flag of the State:** It provides a rectangular flag in shape and red in colour with three equidistant white verticles stripes of equal width, next to the staff and a white plough in the middle with the handle facing the stripes. The ratio of the length of the flag to its width is **3:2** (according to section 144 of the Jammu and Kashmir Constitution)
19. **Official Language:** According to Section 145, the official language of the state shall be Urdu but the English language shall unless the Legislature bylaw otherwise provides, continue to be used for all the official purposes of the state for which it was being used immediate before the commencement of this Constitution.
20. **Academy for Development of Art, Culture and Languages:** The state has established an Academy of Arts, Cultural and Languages for the development of Art and Culture of the State and for the development of Hindi, Urdu and other regional languages of the state.
21. **Appointment of Governor:** After independence, the Governor of the state was known as Sadar-i-Riyasat elected by the State Legislature. But under Section **27,** the Governor is appointed by the President of India by Warrant under his hand and seal. He remains in his office during the pleasure of the President.
22. **Amendment to the State Constitution:** It lays down the procedure of its amendment. It can be amended by a bill passed in each house of the state legislature by a majority of **2/3** of the total membership of that house. Such a bill must be introduced in the assembly only. However, no bill of constitutional amendment can be moved in either House if it seeks to change the relationship of state with the Union of India.
23. Multiparty System: The state enjoys multiparty system which consists of national as well as regional political parties e.g. Congress (I), B.J.P., CPI(M), as national political parties; whereas National Conference, People's Democratic party, Panthers Party, etc. are the regional political parties of the State.

Note:- Moreover, inspite of above written important features of the State Constitution, *The Darbar Movement* can also be kept in it. There are two capitals of the State i.e. Kashmir is the summer capital of the State and Jammu is the winter capital of the State. Every year, in the month of November, the Civil Secretaraite has been shifted from Srinagar to Jammu. And in the similar manner,.it is also shifted from Jammu to Srinagar at the end of April month. It is popularly known as Darbar Move from Brahminism to Dalit history to run the state affair in large scale with the ideology of 'work culture'. (Dr. D.K. Surya; **"History of Chamar Dynasty"** pp. 1-70).

Chapter - 10

Directive Principles of State Politics

Directive Principles in regards to the state Politics are the guidelines to the State Government and the Legislature of the State and all local or other authorities within the territory of the state or under the control of the government of the State. The Constitution of Jammu and Kashmir in Part IV and section 11 to 25 provides the Directive Principles of the State Policy. The Provisions contained in this Part IV are not enforceable by any court but the principles therein laid down are nevertheless fundamental in the governance of the state and it shall be the duty of the state to apply these principles in making laws. (Section 12)

Directive Principles of the State Policy: Jammu and Kashmir

The Constitution of Jammu and Kashmir contains the following Directive Principles of the State Politics = Rajniti + Vedic culture ke History + Chamar. Thought = Ravidas ke Philosophy (Mahar Culture):-

1. **Section 13: State to establish a Socialist Order of Society for the Promotion of Welfare of the People.**

The prime object of the state shall be the promotion of the welfare of the mass of the people by establishing and preserving a socialist order of society wherein all exploitation of man has been abolished and society wherein justice — social, economic and political - shall inform all the institutions of national life-like that of British democracy in India, after 2017.

2. **Section 14: Economy of the state to be Developed in a Planned Manner:** The state shall develop in a planned manner the productive forces of the country with a view to enriching the material and cultural life of the people and foster and protect —
   (a) the public sector where the means of production are owned by the state;
   (b) the co-operative sector where the means of production are cooperatively owned by individuals or groups of individuals; and

(c) the private sector where the means of production are owned by an individual or a corporation employing labour; provided that the operation of this sector is not allowed to result in the concentration of wealth or of the means of production to the common detriment.

3. **Section 15: State to Ensure Speedy Improvement in standard of Living of Rural Masses:** The state shall endeavour to organize and develop agriculture and animal husbandry by bringing to the aid of the cultivator the benefits of modern and scientific research and techniques so as to ensure a speedy improvement in the standard of living as also the prosperity of the rural masses.

4. **Section 16: Organisation of Village Panchayats:** The state shall take steps to organize village Panchayats and endow them with such powers and authority as may be necessary to enable them to function as units of self-government.

5. **Section 17: State to take Certain Steps for Promoting Crafts and Cottage Industries:** The State shall in order to rehabilitate and promote the renowned crafts and cottage industries of the state, initiate and execute well considered programmes for refining and modernizing techniques and modes of production, including the employment of cheap power so that unnecessary drudgery and toil of the workers are eliminated and the artistic value of the products enhanced, while the fullest scope is provided for the encouragement and development of individual talent and initiative.

6. **Section 18: Separation of Judiciary from Executive:** The state shall take steps to separate the judiciary from the executive in the public services, and shall seek to secure a judiciary system which is humane, cheap, certain objective and impartial whereby justice shall be done and shall be seen to be done and shall further strive to ensure efficiency, impartiality and incorruptibility of its various organs of justice, administration and public welfare state.

7. **Section 19: Right to Work and to Public Assistance in Certain Cases:** The State shall within the limits of its economic capacity and development, make effective provision for securing:-

   (a) that all permanent residents, men and women equally, have the right to work, that is the right to receive guaranteed work with payment for labour in accordance with its quantity and quality subject to a basic minimum and maximum wage established by law;

(b) that the health and strength of workers, men and women and the tender age of children are not abused and that permanent residents are not forced by economic necessity to enter avocations unsuited to their sex, age of strength;

(c) that all workers, agricultural, industrial or otherwise, have reasonable just and humane conditions of work with full enjoyment of leisure and social and cultural opportunities;

(d) that all permanent residents have adequate maintenance in old age as well as in the event of sickness disablement, unemployment and other cases of underserved want by providing social insurance, medical aid, hospitals, sanatoria and health resorts at State expenses.

8. **Section 20:** Rights of Free and Compulsory Education in certain cases: The State shall endeavour—

   (a) to secure to every permanent resident, the right to free education upto the University standard;

   (b) to provide, within a period of ten years from the commencement of this Constitution, compulsory education for all children until they complete the age of fourteen years; and

   (c) to ensure to all workers and employees adequate facilities for adult education and part-time technical, professional and vocational courses.

9. **Section 21:** Rights of Children: The state shall strive to secure —

   (a) to all children the right to happy childhood with adequate medical care and attention; and

   (b) to all children and youth equal opportunities in education and employment, protection against exploitation and against moral or material abandonment.

Protection against Exploitation: Children should not be employed in hazardous jobs in factories for manufacture of match boxes and fireworks, and positive steps should be taken for the welfare of such children as well as for improving the quality of their life.

10. **Section 22.** Rights of Women: The state shall endeavour to secure to all women —

   (a) the right to equal pay for equal work;

   (b) the right to maternity benefits as well as adequate medical care in all employments;

(c) the right to reasonable maintenance, extending to cases of married women who have been divorced or abandoned;

(d) the right to full equality in all social, educational, political and legal matters;

(e) special protection against discourtesy, defamation, hooliganism and other forms of misconduct.

11. **Section 23:** Protection of Educational, Material and Cultural Interests of Socially and Economically Backward Sections: The state shall guarantee to the socially and educationally backward sections of the people special care in the promotion of their educational, material and cultural interests and protection against special injustice.

12. **Section 24:** Duty of the State to Improve Public Health: the state shall make every effort to safeguard and promote the health of the people by advancing public hygiene and by prevention of disease through sanitation, pest and vermin control, propaganda and other measures and by ensuring widespread, efficient and free medical services throughout the state and with particular emphasis in its remote and backward regions.

13. **Section 25:** Duty of the State to Foster Equality and Secularism: The state shall combat ignorance, superstition, fanaticism, communalism, racialism, cultural, backwardness and shall seek to foster brotherhood and equality among all communities under the aegis of a Secular State.

Note:- The Drama, origin and principles of this state is based on Dalit philosophy the story of God and man. Traditional values, in nearby future, we have no more = Nagative Islam + Gujjar Missionary Agenda to create sangam literature for the welfare of the Jammu Sate ("William Shakes Peare's Mecbeth", by W. Turner; p. 1. Study the differences of Dalit Christianity and modern Islam = Culprit theory of the Political History of "Kashmir Issue."

Chapter - 11

Panchayati Raj in Jammu and Kashmir

The word 'Panchayat' has been derived from the Sanskrit word '*Panch*' and '*chayat*'. Th former means wise and later means forum for discussion about the Pandava Race of Jammu and Kashmir State. Thus, the word Panchayat is a forum of wise men's discussion of the local problems connected with rural societies = municipal Corporation + NAC, etc.

History reveals the existence of Panchayat system during the Aryan times in India. It was meant for rural agricultural societies of Barnai Dera to cope with basic social justice problems. It was based on the decentralization of power for effective running of the local administration.

Panchayati Raj in Jammu and Kashmir: Before Independence

The history of *Panchayats* in Jammu and Kashmir opened the chapter of Panchayats in the villages in 1935 under the Jammu and Kashmir Panchayat Regulation No. 1 of Samvat 1992 i.e. 1935. These *Panchayats* meant to assist the administration of civil and criminal justice and also to manage the sanitation and other common concerns of the villages. Villages Panchayat Act 1941 was another important act for Panchayat before Independence.

Panchayati Raj in Jammu and Kashmir: After Independence

631 Panchayats were.existed in the state at the time of Independence of India. In 1949 A.D. the department of Panchayats and rural development began its activities for rural upliftment such as improving irrigational arrangement, dewatering the area, bringing waste land under cultivation etc.

Panchayat system envisages three dimensional approaches for all round welfare of the masses with particular stress on individual development of the personality for healthy and prosperous society:-

1. It strengthens the basic roots of democracy which is the best form of government in the world.
2. Through this system, one also gets an opportunity in the decision making process at grass root level.
3. This system enables to oversee and supervise need and requirement based developmental programmes of the local areas for their proper execution.

Jammu and Kashmir Panchayati Raj Act of 1989

Jammu and Kashmir Panchyati Raj Act, 1989 aims at introducing the Panchayati Raj System in a very effective way in Jammu and Kashmir State. The main idea behind this Act is to promote and develop the Panchayati Raj in the state as an important instrument of the local self-government to secure the effective participation of the people in the implementation of the development programmes. This Act, 1989 provides the following authorities:-

1. Halqa Panchayats
2. Block Development Councils
3. District Planning and Development Boards
4. Panchayat Adalats Sarpanch and Panch

1. Halqa Panchayats: J&K panchayati Raj Act, 1989 provides wide ranging powers to the Halqa Panchayat, which is the soul of the system. It is the central around which the planning development and political activities of the people at grass root level revolve,

(a) Composition of Halqa Panchayat: It provides a Halqa Panchayat of every Halqa. Every Halqa Panchayat has the Halqa Majilis comprising of all the persons whose names are including in the electoral roll for such Halqa Panchayat. It consists of "*panches*" not less than seven and not more than eleven including the "*Sarpanch*". The "*Sarpanch*" is elected by the "*Panches*" of the Halqa Panchayat from amongst themselves. The panches are elected from the constituencies. The "*sarpanch*", the "*Naib - sarpanch*" and every "*Panch*" of Halqa Panchayat hold the office for a period of five years from the date of its constitution. Every Halqa Panchayat holds its meeting at least once in a month.

(b) Functions of Halqa Panchayat: The following are some of the important functions of the Halqa Panchayat:-

- to prepare plans for the development of the area and undertake measures for the implementation of the development plans.

- to deal with the problems of soil conservation, water management, social forestry, rural industrialization, agriculture, animal husbandry and sanitation and health.
- to construct and maintain the slaughter houses, regulation of sale and preservation of meat and processing of skins and hide.
- to regulate the building, shops, and entertainment house and checking of offensive or dangerous trades.
- regulation of fairs and festivals.
- preparation and implementation of social developmental plans for alleviating poverty and employment generation through various programmes.
- to involve in implementation of scheme of universalisation of elementary education and other educational programmes Lord Buddha's philosophy or Dalit king Ashoka's view in the composition of the history and Literature.

2. Block Development Council: The Panchayati Raj Act, 1989 provides the constitution of Block Development Council for every block in the state,

(a) Composition of Block Development Council: It consists of the chairman of the Block Development Council. The chairman is indirectly elected through an electoral college consists of sarpanches and the panchas of the panchayats in that block. The government has also the power under this act to nominate two members to give representation to women, SC/other classes.

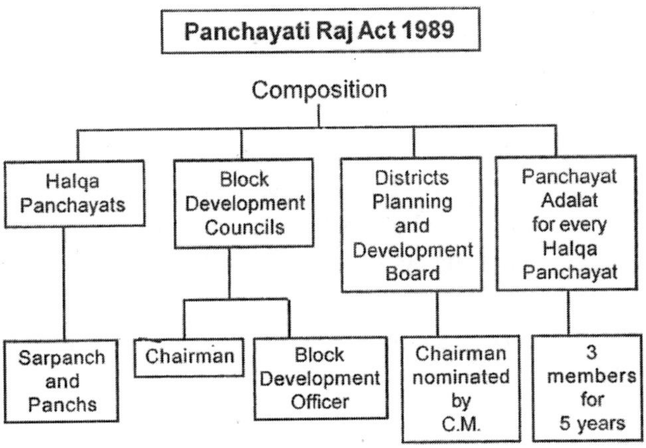

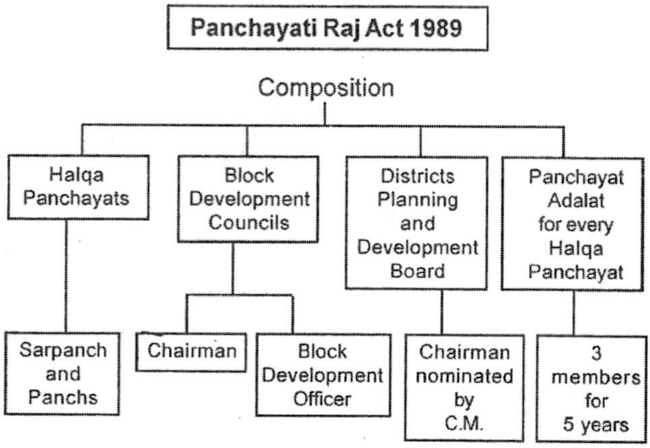

(b) **Functions of Block Development Council:** Its important functions are—

- to construct, maintain and supervise the inter-halqa panchayats communication system
- to provide administration and technical guidance to the Halqa Panchayat and to review its work
- to undertake measures for effective supervision and monitoring of various development programmes which are undertaken by the Halqa Panchayats.
- to supervise plans relating to agriculture, rural development, animal husbandry/sheep husbandry, social forestry, education and public health.
- To supervise and monitor the implementation of poverty alleviation programmes (BPL).
- To carry out such other functions as may be entrusted to it by the government or by District Planning and Development Board.
- For every Block Development Council, there shall be constituted a Block Development Council Fund comprising grants made by the government.
- Every Block Development Council shall .hold its meeting once in a month.

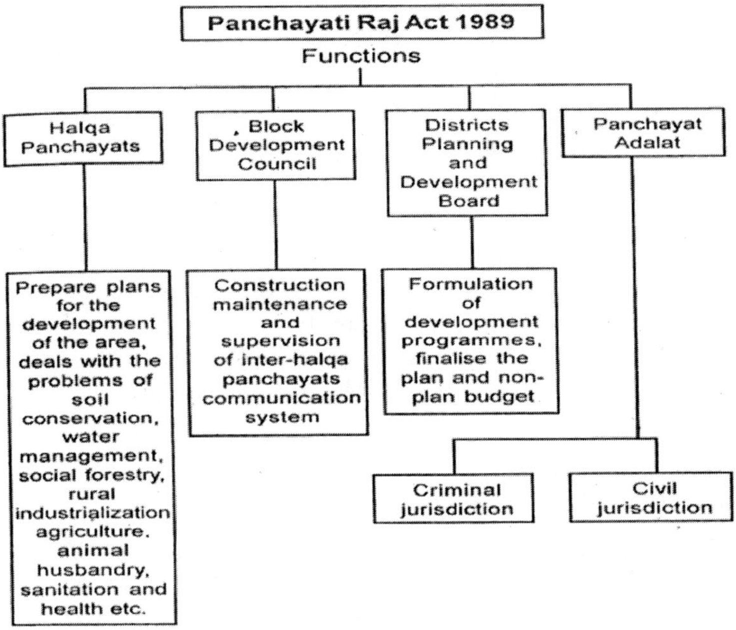

3. District Planning and Development Board: This act also gives the District Planning and Development Board for the proper functioning of the Panchayati Raj system in the state.

(a) **Composition of District Planning and Development Board:** Its chairman is nominated by the Chief-Minister of the State. Chairmen of the Block Development Councils, Town Area committees and Municipal Councils in the District, MLAs and MPs are the ex-officio members of the District Board. The District Development Commissioner's the Chief-Executive of the District Board and he is assigned by the district level heads of the departments in discharging of his functions.

(b) **Functions of the District Board:** The District Planning and Development Board is the highest authority in the power structure of the panchayati raj system. The Board has the following powers and functions —

- to consider and guide the formulation of development programmes for the district and undertake priorities programmes for the district and undertake priorities for various schemes to consider issues relating to the speedy development and economic upliftment of the district,

- to formulate and finalise the plan and non-plan budget,
- to lay down the policy guidelines for the Block Development Council and Halqa Panchayats.
- To review periodically progress and achievement of development plans and schemes and make recommendations as it considers appropriate.
- To function as a working group for formulation of periodic annual plans for the districts.
- To approve the budget of the Block Development Council and supervise and coordinate their work to undertake special measures for alleviating poverty and employment generation.
- To promote and assist cooperation institutions.

4. Panchayat Adalats: This Act 1989 also provides a Panchayat Adalat for every halqa which consists of contiguous numbers of villages as determined by the government.

(a) **Composition of Panchayat Adalat:** The Adalat consists of five members nominated by the prescribed authority out of the panel prepared and recommended by the Halqa Panchayat from its electorate. The term of its member is five years. Three members will form the quorum of the Adalat. The chairman of the Adalat is to be elected by the Adalat from amongst themselves. If they fail to elect witin 15days, the prescribed authority will nominate the chairman. The secretary of the Halqa Panchayat acts as the judicial clerk to the Adalat.

(b) **Functions of the Panchayat Adalat:** According to Panchayati Raj Act, 1989 the Panchayat Adalats enjoy both civil and criminal jurisdictions.

Civil Jurisdiction is confined to claims of the value of Rs .1000.00 involving suits for ascertained sums, for damages for breach of contract not involving immovable property and compensation for wrongful taking or damaging property. The government is empowered to enhance the jurisdiction in civil cases upto Rs. 2000.00.

Criminal Jurisdiction covers a substantial range of offences under the Ranbir Panel code, Samvat 1989 and the special status. These adalats have jurisdiction to try offences such as affray, impersonation of public servant, criminal tresspass, house tresspass, public nuisance including pollution of water, mischief theft etc.

Jammu and Kashmir Panchayati Raj Amendment Act 2004

This act provides panch reservation for the scheduled castes and the scheduled tribes. In every Halqa Panchayat and the number of Panch seats, so reserved, shall bear the same proportion to the total - number of panch seats to be filled by direct election in that Panchayat as the population of SC/ST in that Panchayat area bears to the total population in that area and such Panch seats may be allotted by rotation to different constituencies in a Halqa Panchayat in such manner and by such authority as may be prescribed.

It also states that not less than one-third of the total number of panch seats reserved under above provision shall be reserved for women belonging to the SC/ST.

On July 2, 2016, the J&K Government passed an amendment to Jammu and Kashmir Panchayati Raj Act, 1989, which allows election of Sarpanches by Panches instead of being elected directly. Now, by this amendment, the Sarpanches shall be elected by the people of the state. This amendment also allows to have a single Block Development Council (BDC) for more than one block on the basis of the population, number of Panchayat, Halqa and geography of the area.

Note:- The History of the Dalit Samaj is promoted from zero to hero as top class writers of the World history = Dalit literature. (**"A Primitive History of Untouchables;"** by prof. (Dr.) Ramiyan Bhardwaj; unpublished material: pp. 1-85)

Chapter - 12

Governor of Jammu and Kashmir State = Animal Nature Type of Psychology (N.N. Vohra)

For the peaceful and smooth functioning of the state, the executive powers of the Jammu and Kashmir vest in the Head of the state called as Governor Sh. N.N. Vohra, at present (2017). Prior to the sixth Amendment Act, 1965, the Head of the state was known as '*Sadar-i-Riyasat*' who had to be a permanent resident of the state and indirectly elected by the Legislature. The '*Sadar-i-Riyasat*' could be removed, for the violation of the constitution, by an address in the legislature supported by a majority of not less than two thirds of its total membership, recommending to the President to remove him. After the amendment, this method of removal of the Head of the state has been done away with.

By the constitution of J&K, 6th Amendment Act, 1965, the *Sadar-i-Riyasat* has been substituted by the Governor. Governor is the agent of the Central Government.

Head of the State: Section 26: According to section 26 of the Jammu and Kashmir Constitution, the Head of the state is designated as the Governor. All the executive powers of the state shall be vested in the Governor and shall be exercised by him either directly or through officers subordinate to him in accordance with the constitution.

Appointment of the Governor: Section 27: According to this section, the Governor is appointed by the President of India by warrant under his hand and seal. Narinder Nath Vohra has been appointed as Governor to Jammu and Kashmir by the President of India on 25th June, 2008. (For more details see Appendix VII)

Term of the Office: Section 28: The Governor shall remain in his office during the pleasure of President of India. He shall hold office for a term of five years from the date on which he enters upon his office. He may, by writing under his hand addressed to the President of India, resign his office.

Qualification for the Appointment as Governor: Section 29

1. He must be a citizen of India
2. He has completed the age of 30 years
3. He shall not be a member of either house of Legislature and if a member of either House be appointed as Governor, he shall be deemed to have vacated his seat in the House on the date on which he enters upon his office as 'Governor' (Section 30)
4. He shall not hold any other office of profit (section 30)

Oath of the office: Section 31: The Governor and every **person** discharging the function of the Governor shall before entering **upon** his office, make and subscribe in the presence of the Chief Justice of the High Court or, in his absence, the senior most judge of that court available on oath or affirmation.

Powers of the Governor of Jammu and Kashmir State

The Governor is the agent of the Central Government. His powers can be understood under the following headings:-

1. Executive Powers
2. Legislative Powers
3. Financial Powers
4. Judicial Powers
5. Discretionary Powers
6. Emergency Powers
7. Miscellaneous Powers

1. Executive Powers

(a) The Chief-Minister of the state is appointed by the governor.

(b) On the recommendation of the Chief-Minister, he also appoints other ministers (under section 36). They hold office during the pleasure of the Governor.

(c) He also administers to the Minister or the Deputy Minister the oaths of the Office and of secrecy according to the form set out for the purpose.

(d) He also appoints a judge of the High Court as Advocate General for the state to advise him for legal matters. [Section 42(2)]

(e) He appoints the chairman and other members of the state Public Service Commission.

(f) He can also remove the Chief-Minister and his Council of Ministers from the office.

(g) He is empowered to make rules for the more convenient transaction of the business of the government of the state and for the allocation among Ministers of the said business. (Section 43)

(h) He can dissolve the lower house i.e. the state Legislative Assembly.

(i) He is empowered to nominate not more than two women to be the members of the state Legislative Assembly.

(j) He is also empowered to nominate eight members including three persons belonging to any of the socially or economically backward classes in the state and other five persons having special knowledge or practical experience in respect of matter such as literature, science, art, co-operative movement and social services.

(k) He is informed of all important decisions of the cabinet. (1) He also appoints the Vice-Chancellors of the state Universities.

2. Legislative Powers: Governor enjoys the following legislative powers:

(a) Governor addresses the state Legislative Assembly at the commencement of the first session-after each general election and the first session of each year.

(b) He can send message each House of the Legislative to meet at such time and place as he thinks of it.

(c) He can prorogue the Houses of either House.

(d) He can dissolve the Legislative Assembly and order for fresh elections.

(e) He also appoints speaker and Deputy Speaker to the State Legislative Assembly.

(f) He can appoint any members of the Assembly as speaker when the offices of both the speaker and the Deputy fall vacant.

(g) He can address both the Chambers of the State Legislature independently or collectively.

(h) No bill passed by the Legislature can become an act without his signature.

(i) He can reject the ordinary bill and can reserve certain types of bill for the approval of the President of India.

(j) He can issue Ordinance when the Legislative Assembly is not in session,

(k) He can proclaim emergency due to the failure of the constitutional machinery in the state.

3. Financial Powers

(a) Money bills can be introduced in the Legislative Assembly only with his prior recommendation.

(b) In respect of every financial year, he causes to be laid before both Houses of the Legislature, a statement of the estimated receipts and expenditure of the state. It means that he causes to be laid every year the annual budget in the lower house.

(c) No demand for a grant is made except on the recommendation of the Governor.

(d) The state Contingency Fund is at the disposal of the Governor in which he can make the advance for the purposes of meeting unforeseen expenditure pending authorization of such expenditure by Legislature. In other words, he uses Contingency Fund of the state.

4. Judicial Powers

(a) He appoints a judge of the High Court as the Advocate General for the State.

(b) He gives approval to the Chief Justice for determining the number of judges to sit at Jammu or at Srinagar from time to time.

(c) He makes the appointment, posting and promotion of district judges in consultation with the High Court.

(d) Additional District Judge and Session Judges etc. are also appointed by him. He has to consult the High Court for such appointments.

(e) According to Section 34 of J&K Constitution, the Governor has the judiciary to grant pardons, reprieves, respites or remissions of punishment or to suspend, remit or commute the sentence of any person convicted of any offence against any law relating to a matter to which the executive power of the state extends.

(f) On the basis of section 110 of the J&K Constitution, the Governor makes the appointments of persons other than district judges to the judicial services of the state in accordance with the rules made by him in that behalf after consultation with the Public Service Commission and with the High Court.

5. Discretionary Powers: The Governor enjoys the following discretionary powers—

(a) He may refuse or give assent to a bill or he may send it back for reconsideration by the State Legislature. He may even reserve a bill for the consideration of the President.

(b) According to Article 356, the Governor of a state may send a report to the centre that the state government is not functioning in accordance with the provisions of the Constitution. In such a situation, the President's Rule is imposed in the state and the Governor's powers are enhanced.

(c) If no party gets majority in the Legislative Assembly, the Governor uses his discretion in selecting the Chief-Minister.

(d) If a Government loses majority in th Legislative Assembly and does not resign, the Governor can dismiss the government. He may or may not dissolve the Legislative Assembly.

(e) When no political party is in a position to form coalition government, under such condition, he can also use his discretionary powers to impose Governor rule e.g. he used his discretionary power while imposing Governor rule from 9th January 2016 to 8 March 2016.

(f) The Governor can remove the Chief-Minister of the State in case he feels that the government does not enjoy the confidence of the majority or is not working properly as it was done by the governor of the state Mr. Jag Mohan in July 1984 when he removed CM. Farooq Abdullah.

6. Emergency powers

Role of Governor as an Agent of Central government: Section 92 of the Jammu and Kashmir Constitution:

In relation to states other than Jammu and Kashmir, the Constitution of India empowers to President to take action on the report received from the Governor of a State. So far as Jammu and Kashmir State is concerned although the Union Government is obliged to ensure that the Government of the State is carried on in accordance with the provisions of the Indian Constitution on the grounds of failure of the constitutional machinery in the state.

Section 92 of the Jammu and Kashmir constitution states the provisions in case of the failure of constitutional machinery in the state.

Section 92.

1. If at any time, the Governor is satisfied that a situation has arisen in which the Government of the State cannot be carried on in accordance with the provisions of this Constitution, the Governor may by Proclamation—

(a) Assume to himself all or any of the functions of the Government of the State and all or any of the powers vested in or exercisable by anybody or authority, in this state;

(b) Make such incidental and consequential provisions as appear of the Governor to be necessary or desirable for giving effect to the objects of the Proclamation, including provisions for suspending in whole or in part the operation of any provision of this constitution relating to anybody or authority in the state:—

1. Provided that nothing in this section shall authorize the Governor to assume to himself any of the powers vested in or exercisable by the High Court or to suspend in whole or in part the operation of any provision of this constitution relating to the High Court = over dated constitution of India.
2. Any such proclamation may be revoked or varied by a subsequent proclamation.
3. Any such proclamation whether varied under sub-section (2) or not shall except where it is a proclamation revoking a previous proclamation, cease to operate on the expiration of six months from the date on which it was first issued.
4. If the Governor by a proclamation_under this section assumes to himself any of the powers of the Legislature to make laws, any law made by him in the exercise of that power shall, subject to the terms thereof, continue to have effect until two years have elapsed from the date on which the proclamation ceases to have effect, unless sooner repealed or re-enacted by an Act of the Legislature, and any reference in this constitution to any Acts of or laws made by the Legislature shall be construed as including a reference to such law.
5. No proclamation under sub-section (1) shall be issued except with the concurrence of the President of India.

6. Every proclamation under this section shall, except where it is a proclamation revoking a previous proclamation be laid before each House of the Legislature as soon as it is convened.

Section 92 empowers the Governor to assume to himself all or any of the functions of the executive, legislature or the power vested in or exercisable by any authority in the state. Such a power can be exercised only after the Governor is satisfied about the existence of special situation making it impossible for carrying on the functioning of the state Govt, in accordance with the constitution. Such an exercise is commonly known as the imposition of the Governor's Rule in the state. The proclamation issued under this section is only for 6 months. No proclamation imposing the Governor Rule can be issued except with the concurrence of the President of India, A proclamation issued under sub section (1) is required to be laid before each house of the Legislature as soon as it is convened. The proclamation issued by the Governor, can be revoked or varied by a subsequent proclamation. The Governor has been empowered to issue incidental and consequential orders for giving effect to the objects of proclamation. He can suspend in whole or in part the operation of any provision of Constitution including the fundamental rights. The term proclamation signifies a public announcement and this requirement would be satisfied when the problem is published in the Government Gazzette.

7. Miscellaneous Powers

(a) **Chairman of the Shri Amarnathji Shrine Board:** Governor of the state, if a Hindu, is an ex-officio chairman of the Shri Amarnathji Shrine Board and if a non-Hindu, he has to nominate an eminent person of the state professing Hindu religion.

(b) **Chancellor of the Universities of State:** Governor is the chancellor of the state Universities and the Central Universities of the Jammu and Kashmir. The Vice-chancellors of the State Universities are appointed by the Governor e.g. Governor to J&K state Mr. N.N. Vohra has appointed Dr. R.D. Sharma as the vice-chancellor of University of Jammu, Jammu.

Note:- After the death of Dr. B.R. Ambedkar, there was a strong Brahminism widely spread in India, and the next VC of this state will be R.D. Sharma as a local and honest article of this state without knowledge; but at the same time, he has no knowledge of the Dalit History = Names Like S.P. Salinder Singh, Dilbag Singh and so on = Dalit literature = Honest living Approach. (F. Singh: Honest Living = Farmar Study literature = Labour Concept; pp. 1-102)

Chapter - 13

Chief Minister and Council of Ministers

Chapter VI entitled "Instrument of Accession = New Constitution of India & Dalit History of the State" and note: Constitution of Jammu and Kashmir deals with the powers of the Governor, Council of Ministers and Chief Minister of the state. The council of Ministers is the main executive organ of the government and its stability is essential for the efficient running of the administration but at the same time (2017 to 2018) there is turmoil in the state on the regions propaganda. Section 35 states that there shall be council of ministers with one Chief-Minister at the head to aid and advise the Governor in the exercise of his function. All functions of the Governor except those under sections 36, 38 and 92 shall be exercised by him only on the advice of the Council of Ministers but there is no efficiency found in executing the power of ministers.

Chief Minister of Jammu and Kashmir: Powers and Position

The chief Minister of the state is the real executive head of the government machinery, although formally the Governor enjoys the executive authority. Hence, the Governor is the head of the state and the Chief-Minister is the head of the government. He enjoys a very unique position in the state administration = anti-Dalit propaganda.

Qualification

(i) He must be the permanent resident of the state.

(ii) He must be a member of the state Legislature.

(iii) If he/she is not a member of state Legislature. He/she has to be elected to either house within a period of six months.

(iv) He must complete the age of twenty-five year.

(v) He must not hold any office of profit.

(vi) He must such other qualifications as may be prescribed in that behalf by or under any law made by legislature.

Appointment

The leader of the majority party or coalition partners is appointed as the Chief-Minister of the state by the Governor. To cite an example Governor S.K. Sinha appointed Ghulam Nabi Azad as the CM. of the state on 2nd Nov. 2005. Governor N.N. Vohra appointed N.C. leader Omar Abdullah as the CM. of the state on 5th January 2009. Now again Governor Narinder Nath Vohra appointed PDP leader Mufti Mohd. Sayeed as the CM. of the state on 9th March, 2015 supported by Bhartiya Janta Party (coalition partners). Now, after the death of Mufti Mohd. Sayeed, he appointed his daughter Ms Mehbooba Mufti as Chief-Minister of the State. (For more details see Appendix VIII).

Tenure

According to Section 52 of the Jammu and Kashmir, the Legislative Assembly shall continue for six years from the date appointed for its first meeting and no longer and the expiration of the said period of six years shall operate as a dissolution of the Assembly.

Thus, the Chief-Minister can remain in his office for the period of six years. He holds office till the time he has majority in the legislature.

Powers and Functions of Chief-Minister

Chief-Minister of the state enjoys the following powers and functions:-

1. Link between Council of Ministers and Governor
2. Powers in Relation to Council of Ministers
3. Powers and Functions in Relation to the state Legislature
4. Miscellaneous

1. Link between Council of Ministers and Governor: Chief-Minister is a link between the Council of Ministers and Governor. According to section 44 of the state constitution—

(a) The Chief Minister communicates the Governor all decisions of the Council of Ministers relating to the administration of the affairs of the state and proposals for legislation,

(b) All powers exercised by the Governor are in reality exercised by the Chief-Minister.

2. Powers in Relation to the Council of Ministers

(a) Other ministers are appointed by the Governor on the recommendation of the Chief-Minister.

(b) He distributes the portfolios to his ministers

(c) He guides, directs, controls and co-ordinates the activities of other ministers.

(d) He can ask any minister to resign. If the minister does not resign, he can ask the Governor to dismiss him.

(e) He reshuffles his cabinet.

(f) He presides over the meetings of his Council of Ministers.

(g) He coordinates the working of various departments in the formulation and implementation of policy.

(h) Thus, he is the leader and chairman of the Council of Ministers.

3. Powers and Functions in Relations to the State Legislature

(a) The sessions of the house are summoned and prorogued by the Governor on the advice of the CM.

(b) The agenda of the house is determined by the speaker in consultation with the Chief-Minister.

(c) All important principal appointments are made by the CM. in the State Legislative Assembly.

(d) He makes services rules.

(e) He makes important changes in the administrative system of the state.

(f) He prepares development projects for state.

(g) He advises the Governor over the dissolution of the State Legislative Assembly also.

(h) Thus, he is the leader of the State Legislative Assembly also.

4. Miscellaneous

(a) He is the leader of the people of the state.

(b) He is the chief spokesman of the state Government.

(c) He is the principal adviser of the Governor.

(d) He is the chairman of Haj Committee of Jammu and Kashmir.

Council of Ministers

The council of Ministers is formed by the Chief-Minister of the state. The Governor appoints various Ministers on the recommendation of the Chief Ministers of the state. There is no fixed term of office prescribed for the ministers. He holds office during the pleasure of the Governor. As a member of Council of Ministers, a minister is collectively or individually responsible to the State Assembly. The Governor can dismiss a minister on the advice of the Chief-Minister.

The size of the Council of Ministers is not uniform. It has been left to the discretion of the CM. who determines it. It has been observed that the size of the council of ministers has been increasing particularly in a coalition government. After the Assembly Election 2015, a coalition government of PDP and B.J.P. had formed in J&K state. The Council of Ministers of J&K states consisted of 19 Cabinet Ministers and 6 Ministers of State.

Council of Ministers (J&K State) 2015-16

Cabinet ministers	Department
1. Mr. Mufti Mohd, Sayeed	Honourable Chief-Minister J&K, Home, Tourism, GAD, Information, Estate and Planning.
2. Dr. Nirmal KumarSingh	Deputy CM., Power Development Housing and Urban Development
3. Mr. Abdul Rehman Veeri	Horticulture and Haj Auqaf.
4. Mr. Chander Prakash Ganga	Industries and commerce
5. Mr. Javaid Mustafa Mir	Revenue.
6. Mr. Lal Singh	Health and Medical Education, ARI and Training
7. Mr. Abdul Haq Khan	**Rural Development**
8. Mr. Bali Bhagat	Social welfare, forest, Ecology and Environment.
9. Syed Basharat Ahmed Bukhari	Law, Justice and Parliamentary Affairs & Relief Rehabilitation.
10. Mr. Sukhanandan Kumar	Public Health Engineering, Irrigation and Flood Control
11. Choudhary Zulfkar Ali	Consumer Affairs & Public Distribution & Tribal Affairs.
12. Mr. Sjad Gani Lone	Science & Technology & Animal Husbandry.
13. Mr. Hasseb A. Drabu	Finance, Labour & Employment and Culture.
14. Mr. Ghulan Nabi Lone	Agriculture Production
15. Mr. Imran Raza Ansari	Information Technology, Technical Education and Youth Services & Sports
16. Syed Mohd. Altaf Bukhari	Public works,. Floriculture, Gardens and Parks.
17. Mr.NaeemAkhtar	Education.
18. Mr. Abdul Gani Kohli	Transport, Rural Development and Horticulture
19. Mr. CheringDorjay	Co-opertive (Independent charge) and Ladakh Affairs.

Ministers of State	
1. Mr. Abdul Majid Padder	Public Health Engineering, Irrigation and Flood Control, Animal Husbandry and Forest
2. Mr. Sunil Kumar Sharma	Public works (R&B) & Revenue
3. Mr. Mohammad Ashraf Mir	Industries & Commerce, Power Development & Housing & Urban Development.

(Contd...)

4. Ms. Priya Sethi	Information, Education and Culture
5. Mr. Pawan Kumar Gupta	Finance and Information Technology
6. Ms. Asiya Naqash	Health and Social Welfare

After the death of J&K Chief Minister, Mufti Mohammad Sayeed, her daughter Ms Mehbooba Mufti became the first woman Chief Minister of the state on 4th April, 2016. She has reshuffled her Council of Ministers.

The following members enjoying different portfolios:

Cabinet ministers	Department
1. Ms Mehbooba Mufti:	Honourable Chief Minister, J&K State, Home, Tourism, GAD, Information, Estate, Planning Tourism.
2. Dr. Nirmal Kumar Singh:	Deputy Chief Minister and Minister for Power Development and Housing and Urban Development.
3. Mr. Abdul Rehman Veeri:	Minister for Pubic Works and Parliament Affairs.
4. Mr. Chander Prakash Ganga:	Industries and Commerce
5. Mr. Ghulam Nabi Lone:	Agriculture Production
6. Mr. Bali Bhagat:	Health and Medical Education.
7. Mr. Abdul Haq Khan:	Rural Development and Panchayati Raj and Law and Justice.
8. Mr. Lal Singh:	Forest, Ecology and Environment.
9. Mr. Syed Basharat Ahmed Bukhari:	Revenue, Relief and Rehabilitation.
10. Mr. Sayad Gani Lone:	Social Welfare, ARI & Trainings and Science & Technology.
11. Mr. Haseeb A. Drabu:	Finance, Culture and Labour & Employment.
12. Mr. Chering Dorjay:	Cooperatives and Ladakh Affairs.
13. Chowdhery Zulfar Ali:	Consumer Affairs & Public Distribution.
14. Mr. Sham Lai Choudhary:	PHE, Irrigation and Flood Control.
15. Mr. NaeemAkhtar:	Education to R&B.
16. Mr. Abdul Ghani Kohli:	Animal, Sheep Husbandry and Fisheries.
17. Mr. Imran Raza Ansari:	Information Technology, Technical Education and Youth Services & Sports Youth.

Ministers of State	
1. Ms. Asiea Naqash :	Housing & Urban Development Social Welfare, Health & Medical Education.
2. Mr. Sushil Kumar Sharma:	Transport (Independent Charge), Revenue, Public Works (Roads & Buildings), Rural Development & Panchayati Raj, Agriculture Production, YSS.
3. Mr. Farooq Ahmed Andrabi:	Haj and Auqaf (Independent Charge), PHE & Irrigation & Flood Control, Power Development, Industries & Commerce.
4. Smt Priya Sethi:	Education, Technical Education, Culture, Tourism, Horticulture, Floriculture and Parks.

(*Contd...*)

5. Mr. Zahoor Ahmed Mir:	Forest, Ecology and Environment, Animal & Sheep Husbandary, Cooperative and Fisheries.
6. Mr. Ajay Nanda:	Finance and Planning, Information Technology, Law, Justice and Parliamentary Affairs, CA and PD, Tribal Affairs, Relief & Rehabilation and L & Emp.

Kavinder Gupta is the Speaker and Nazir Ahmed Gurezi is the Deputy Speaker of J&K State Legislative Assembly.

Powers and Functions of Council of Ministers

The powers and functions of Council of Ministers can be understood under following headings:-

1. Council of Ministers and the Governor
2. Relations Between the Council of Ministers and the State Legislature
3. Its Important Functions

1. Councils of Ministers and the Governor

(a) **Aid and Advise to the Governor-**section 35 of the J&K constitution states that there shall be a council of ministers with one Chief-Minister at head to aid and advise the Governor in the exercise of his functions.

(b) All functions of the Governor except those under section 36, 38 and 92 shall be exercised by him only on the advice of the Council of Ministers.

(c) All members of Council of Ministers are appointed by the Governor on the recommendation of the Chief-Minister.

(d) All ministers and the Deputy Ministers shall hold office during the pleasure of the Governor.

(e) All the decisions of the Council of Ministers are communicated to the Governor by the Chief Minister.

2. Relations Between the Council of Ministers and the State Legislature

(a) Council of Ministers is collectively responsible to the State Legislative Assembly.

(b) The Council of Ministers remains the office so long as it enjoys the confidence of the State Legislative Assembly.

3. Important Functions of Council of Ministers

(a) The formulation and determination of the policies of the state are the most important functions of the council of ministers

(b) It runs the state administration in accordance with the policies of the government.

(c) It is the responsibility of the Council of Ministers to secure coordination in the working of various governmental departments.

(d) It also makes all important appointments in the state.

(e) It plays a significant role in the law-making processes.

(f) It controls the finances of the state. It formulates and implements all developmental policies and plans. The Finance Minister is responsible for preparing and presenting the budget.

Note:- Present Assembly is based on their Negativism, Dalits, they are debarred from the political rights, it has already been mentioned in various books of the author to clear the picture of the state in formal study. Informally, they are strong people of this area as original race of the Pandava Kumba of Dera Barnai (Jammu) in the story of drafting the Dalit-literature for the coming generation.

Chapter - 14

State Legislature

Historical Background

The State of Jammu and Kashmir had a Legislative Assembly called the Praja Sabha during the Dogra Rule of Maharaja Hari Singh it was the begining was the Brahminism in the State. It was established in 1934. It was the first step towards the establishment of a separate legislature in the state. The constitution of Jammu and Kashmir of 1939 provided for a unicameral legislature comprising of His Highness and the Praja Sabha. The power of this Assembly was very limited but it had some control over the executive. It was nursery for the training of the legislature. Later on, it did not function in Kashmir at the commencement of the Constitution of India. The Constitution of Jammu and Kashmir came into existence on 26th January, 1957 which provided bicameral legislature. Part VI and section 46 of the J&K Constitution deal with the State Legislature.

Section 46 state, "There shall be a legislature for the state which shall consist ofthe Governor, and two Houses to be known respectively as the Legislative Assembly and the Legislative Council."

Composition of Legislative Assembly

According to section 47 of the J&K Constitution, the Legislative Assembly shall consist of one hundred and eleven members chosen by the direct election from territorial constituencies in the state. Again on the basis of section 47, if the Governor is of the opinion that women are not adequately represented in the Assembly, he may nominate not more than two women to be members of the Legislative Assembly.

According to Section 48,24 seats in the Legislative Assembly shall remain vacant for the members belonging to the state's territory occupied by Pakistan. It shall not be taken into account for reckoning the total membership of the Assembly. Thus, the total strength of state Legislative Assembly is 87 (see appendix IX).

Election

The members of the Legislative Assembly are directly elected by the permanent residents of the state on the basis of adult sufferage (Section 140 of the J&K constitution).

Qualifications for the Membership of the Legislature

Section 51 of the State Constitution provides the qualifications for the membership of the legislatures in the following ways:-

(h) He must be a Permanent Resident of the State

(i) He must have completed the age of 25 years.

(j) He must possess such other qualifications as may be prescribed in that behalf by or under any law made by Legislature.

(k) He must not hold any office of profit.

(1) He must not be of unsound mind and should not have been declared disqualified by the competent court on the ground of non-residence crime or corrupt or illegal practice (Section 140 of J&K Constitution).

Duration of Legislative Assembly

It is temporary house. According to Section 52 of the J&K Constitution, the duration of the Legislative Assembly is six year. Its term begins from the date appointed for its first meeting Assembly stands automatically dissolved after the expiry of six years. The Governor is empowered to dissolve the Assembly even before the expiry of its term.

Quorum According to section 65 of the J&K Constitution, the quorum to constitute a meeting of the Legislative Assembly shall be of twenty members.

Officers of the state Legislature

Section 57 of the J&K Constitution empowers the Legislative Assembly to choose two members of the Assembly to the respectively Speaker and Deputy Speaker.

Salaries and allowances of the Members of State Legislative Assembly

Section 73 of the State Constitution states - "Members of the Legislative

Assembly and the Legislative Council shall be entitled to receive such salaries and allowances as may from time to time be determined by Legislature by law and until provision in that respect is so made, salaries and allowances at such rates and upon such conditions as were immediately before the commencement of this constitution applicable in the case of members of the Constituent Assembly.

Powers and Functions of the state Legislative Assembly

The following are some of the important powers and functions of the state Legislative Assembly:-

1. Legislative Functions
2. Financial functions
3. Electoral Functions
4. Control over Executive

1. **Legislative Functions:** The state Legislative Assembly is empowered to make laws on all subjects contained in the state list and the concurrent list. The bills passed by the State Legislative Assembly become laws after the signature of the Governor. In case, a law made by the state Legislature on a Concurrent Subject comes into conflict with a Union Law on the same subject, the Indian Parliament is empowered to make laws on the Concurrent Law.
2. **Financial Functions:** The State Legislative Assembly has the powers to levy taxes in respect of all subjects of the state list. It is the custodian of the finances of state. No revenue can be collected or tax can be levied or collected by the State Government without the consent of the State Legislature. The budget and all other financial policies and programmes of the State Government becomes effective and operational only after getting an approval from the state legislature. During emergency, the financial powers are exercised by the Union Parliament.

3. **Electoral Functions**

(a) The members of the State Legislative Assembly participate in the election of the President of India.

(b) They also elect the representatives of the state for the Rajya Sabha.

(c) Certain constitutional amendments are made by the India Parliament only with the ratification of the half of the State Legislatures.

(d) State Legislature also elects its Speaker and Deputy Speaker amongst its members e.g., Kavinder Gupta is the speaker to the State Legislative Assembly.

4. Control over Executive: State Legislative Assembly controls the working of the Executive. The State Council of Ministers in collectively responsible to the Legislative Assembly. Actually, Council of Ministers and Chief-Minister run the government with the support of Assembly. Otherwise a motion of vote of non-confidence against the Executive can fall the Government.

Composition of State Legislative Council

Jammu and Kashmir State has a bicameral legislature i.e. State Legislative Council as upper House and State Legislative Assembly as Lower House.

Composition: According to section 50 of J&K Constitution the state Legislative Council consists of 36 members. Out of 36 members —

1. Eleven members are elected by the members of the -Legislative Assembly from amongst persons who are residents of the province of Kashmir and are not members of the Legislative Assembly. Among these 11 members, at least one should be a resident of Ladakh and at least one should be a resident of Kargil.
2. Eleven members are elected by the members of the Legislative Assembly from amongst persons who are residents of the province of Jammu and are not members of the Legislative Assembly. Among these 11 members, one must be a resident of Doda and another must be resident of Poonch.
3. One members is elected by each of the following electorates namely-—
   (a) The members of municipal council, town area committee and notified area committee in the province of Kashmir;
   (b) The members of municipal council, town area committees and notified area committee in the province of Jammu.
4. One teacher of Kashmir province and one teacher of Jammu province.
5. Two members are elected by each of the following electorates namely—
   (a) The members of the Panchayats and such other local bodies in the Province of Kashmir.

(b) The members of the Panchayats and such other local bodies in the Province of Jammu.

6. Eight members are nominated by Governor, not more than three of whom are the persons belonging to any of the socially or economically backward classes in the State, and the others are persons having special knowledge or practical experience in respect of matters such as literature, science, art, co-operative movements and social service.

Hence, the Legislative Council provides an opportunity for persons of intellectual capacity and experience of affairs to help the state with their experience and knowledge.

Qualifications M.A. M.Phil. Ph.D.

1. He must be the Permanent Resident of the state.
2. He must complete the age of 30 years.
3. He must possess such other qualifications as may be prescribed in that behalf by or under any law made by Legislature.
4. He must not hold any office of profit.
5. He must not be of unsound mind and should not have been declared disqualified by the competent court on the ground of non-residence, crime or corrupt or illegal practice.

Duration of the Legislative Council

State Legislative Council is a permanent house. Thus, it is not to be subject to dissolution. One-third of the members retire every second years. The duration of an individual members is six years. The retiring members are eligible for re-elections.

Quorum

According to section 65 of Jammu and Kashmir Constitution, the quorum for the meeting of state Legislative council is of 10 members.

Officers of the State Legislative Council

Section 61 of the J&K Constitution empowers the State Legislative Council to choose its two members as the Chairman and Deputy Chairman. They preside over the session of the Council.

Powers and Functions of the State Legislative Council

The state Legislative Council is the Upper House of the State Legislature. It is a very weak chamber. It exercises minor and .limited powers—

1. Legislative Powers
2. Financial Powers
3. Control Over the Executive

1. Legislative Powers: An ordinary or non-money bill can be introduced in either House of the state Legislature. It is required to be passed by both the Houses for becoming a law. If the bill is moved in the Legislative Assembly in the first instance and it goes to the council after having been passed by the Assembly, the Council has 4 alternatives before it—

(a) It may pass the bill
(b) It may reject the bill
(c) It may amend the bill
(d) It may not take any action on it.

In case of (b) (c) and (d), the Legislative Assembly considers the bill for the second time, but it may or may not accept the amendments made by the Council and repass the bill as it is.

The Council cannot delay the bill for more than one month for the second time.

2. Financial Powers: The Upper House has very limited powers in the financial matters. Financial bill, passed by the Assembly, is sent to the Council for its recommendation. The Council is required to return it with 14 days. It can make certain suggestions but it is for the Assembly to accept these or not.

3. Control Over the Executive: The State Legislative Council has little control over the Executive because the Council of Ministers is responsible to the Assembly alone. The Legislative Council exercises some control over the state Ministry by asking questions and supplementary questions to the Ministers for settlement of "Kashmir Issue" = Dalit-literature.

Chapter -15

Judicial System of Jammu and Kashmir

Judicial power is the element of sovereignty concerned with the application of the laws. The judiciary in Jammu and Kashmir acts as the interpreter and guardian of the Constitution. The first High Court was established in J&K state on 28th March 1928 with a Chief Justice and two other judges. Lala Kanwar Sain was appointed as the first Chief Justice of the Court whereas Rai Bahadur Lala Bodu Raj Sawhney and Khan Sahib Agah Syed Hussain were two other judges. It was the highest judicial body in the State, although, appeal from it lay to High Highness.

Composition of the High Court

Part VII and Section 93 of the Jammu and Kashmir Constitution deal with the composition of High Court.

Section 93 states—The High Court of Jammu and Kashmir consists of a Chief-Justice and two or more other judges. The Constitution does not fix any maximum number of judges, but provides that the minimum numbers of judges of the High Court, excluding the Chief-Justice at any time, will be two. The present strength of the High Court is 14 judges, including 9 permanent Judges and 5 Additional Judges. High Court officiates in Srinagar from May to October end and in Jammu from November to April end. Thus, court sections of both Jammu and Srinagar wings of the High Court functions through out the year. Presently, N. Paul Vasantha Kumar is the Chief Justice of High Court of Jammu and Kashmir (For more details see appendix X).

Appointment of the Judges of the High Court

The appointment of the judges is made by the President of India with the consultation of the following persons:-

1. Chief-Justice of India = Nam

2. The Governor
3. Chief-Justice of Kashmir

In case of the appointment of the Chief-Justice ofKashmir, the Chief-Justice of India and the Governor are consulted by the President of India.

Qualification of the Judges of the High Court

A candidate for the appointment of judge of the High Court must be fulfilled the following qualifications:

1. He must be a citizen of India
2. He must have held judicial office in the state or in any part of India at least for 10 years.
3. Or he must have been an advocate of the High Court **of** Kashmir or of any other High Court in India or of two or more such courts in succession.

Duration of the Judges of the High Court

Judges of the High Court remain in their offices upto the age of 62. It means that 62 years is the retirement age of the judges of the High Court.

Removal of the Judges

A judge of the High Court may resign his office by writing under his hand addressed to the President of India. The removal of the judges of the state High Court can only be made after an address for their removal supported and passed by the parliament of India on the grounds of "proved misbehavior or incapacity" and presented to the President in accordance with Article 124(4) of the Constitution oflndia.

Powers and Jurisdiction of High Court = nil/nil Historical Research.

The jurisdictions of High Court of Jammu and Kashmir can be understood under the following two headings—

I. Legal Jurisdictions
II. Administrative Jurisdictions

I. Legal Jurisdictions of High Court of J&K state:

Independence of Judiciary is the most important basic feature of the Constitution. J&K Constitution has also empowered the High.

Court the following legal jurisdictions:-

1. **Original Jurisdictions:** High Court has jurisdiction to hear and determine any original suit or other proceeding of which the value is not less than Rs 20000/- and every such suit or proceeding shall be instituted in the High Court.
2. **Appellate Jurisdictions:** Appeals from the lower courts lies to the High Court and the procedure for filing these appeals etc. are the appellate jurisdictions of high Court. High Court has jurisdiction to entertain and dispose of such appeals, revision and other cases civil, criminal and revenue, as it may be empowered to do under any enactment in force in the state.
3. **Advisory Jurisdictions:** High Court has also empowered by the advisory jurisdictions. The Governor of the state may take the advices of the High Court while exercising his judicial powers under section 34 of the Jammu and Kashmir Constitution.
4. **Judicial Review:** The High Court can exercise the power of judicial review. The High Court can take any strict action against the order of the government if it violates any provision of the constitution.
5. **Court of Record:** The High Court is a court of record. It is a superior court in the state which is itself competent to determine the scope of its jurisdictions. A court of record means the records which are produced before any court, are not be questioned.
6. **Powers to Punish for Contempt:** It means that when the High Court is vested with the j jurisdiction to punish such contemnors, it is matter lying entirely at the absolute discretion of the High Court either to take or not to take any proceedings in this behalf.
7. **Contempt of Court:** It is disobedience of the Court by acting in opposition to the authority, justice and dignity thereof. It signifies a willful disregard or disobedience of the court's order. It also signifies such conduct as tends to bring the authority of the Court and the administration of law into dispute.
8. **Power to Issue certain Writs:** Section 103 of the Jammu and Kashmir Constitution empowers the High Court to issue to any person or authority or government, the directions, order or writs including writs in the nature of Habeas Corpus, Mandamus, Prohibition, Quo-Warrants, Certiorari or any of them, for any purpose other than those mentioned in clause (2A) of Article 32 of the Indian Constitution.

9. **Seal of the High Court:** The seal of the High Court is used when the occasion may require and has to be kept in the custody of the Registrar or such other officers of the Court as the Chief-Justice may designate. It is aimed at authenticity of the orders issued in the name of the High Court.

II. Administrative Jurisdictions.

1. The High Court is empowered to superintend and control over all subordinate courts.
2. All appointments of the officers and servants of the High Court are made by the Chief-Justice of High Court.
3. Appointment of persons, the posting and promotions of district judges in the state are made by the Governor in consultation with the High Court. (Section 109)
4. Appointments of persons other than district judges to the judicial service of the state are made by Governor in accordance with rules made by him in that behalf after consultation with the PSC and with the High Court (Section 110)
5. The High Court is empowered to control over district court, subordinate courts including the posting, promotion, grant to leave etc. (Section 111)
6. The High Court may call for returns from subordinate courts.
7. High Court makes and issues general rules and prescribed forms for regulating the practice and proceedings of such courts.
8. It also prescribes forms in which books, entries and accounts are kept by the officers of any such court.
9. The High Court also settle tables of fees to be allowed to the sheriff and all clerks and officers of such courts and to attorneys, advocates etc.

Chapter - 16

Party System in Jammu and Kashmir = Progressive Idea of Dalit-literature

Political party system is a significant phenomena of every politics. No democrate political system work without political parties. The struggle for power revolves round the political parties in every democratic political system- party system is a bridge between the government and general masses. It conveys the grievances of people is the administration and helps in the decision-making processes. Political parties are considered as the life lines of modern politics. Political parties keep the democracy alive in the state. Party system brings awareness among the people of the state, formal Samaj to informal Samaj.

Jammu and Kashmir state has the following important features of the party system:—

1. **One Dominant Party System: National Conference:** One political party i.e. Jammu and Kashmir National Conference has played a dominant role in the state politics of Jammu and Kashmir. Since its formation in 1938, it enjoyed a popular support from the people of the state because of its fight for the freedom of the state. Its founder father Sheikh Mohammad Abdullah remained the Prime-Minister since 5th March 1948 to 9th August, 1953. Again this party remained in power under the prime-ministership of Bakshi Ghulam Mohammad and Kliwaja Shans-ud-Din upto 29th February 1964. Later on, from 1975-1984, the political power was enjoyed by Sheikh Mohd. Abdullah and Dr. Farroq Abdullah respectively. Again the Farooq Government remained in power from 1986 to 1990. State was under the president's rule since January 1990 to October 1996. During 1996 state legislative election, NC formed the government under the leadership of Farooq Abdullah upto 18th Oct 2002. During 2008 State Assembly

Election, Omar Abdullah formed MC-Cong I coalition government on 5th January 2009 to 8th January 2015. Hence, NC has been enjoyed the political power for 46 years since after independence.

2. **Multiparty System:** Multiparty system is operating Jammu and Kashmir state. There are number of national as well as regional political parties such as
   (a) National Political Parties:
   - Indian National Congress i.e. Cong (I).
   - Bhartiya Janta Party (BJP)
   - Communist Party of India CPI - (M)
   - Bahujan Samaj Party (BSP)

   (b) Regional Political Parties:
   - All Jammu and Kashmir National Conference (NC)
   - People's Democratic Party (PDF)
   - J&K National Panthers Party » People's Democratic Front
   - J&K Democratic Party Nationalist
   - People's Conference.
3. **Lack of clear Ideologies Among Political Parties**: All political parties of the state have the same ideologies based on socialism, secularism, democracy, decentralization, removal of poverty etc. There is lack of ideological differences. Thus, the members of a political party donot hesitate to switch their loyalties from one party to another. To cite an example, Mufti Mohammad Sayeed formed his regional political party in 1999-PDP- after remaining the active leader and minister of congress Government and V.P. Singh's Jana Morcha Government. Leaving Congress I and joining B.J.P by Choudhary Lal Singh during 10th Jammu and Kashmir State Legislative Assembly Election 2014 is another example.
4. **Personality Politics:** Personality politics also dominates party politics in the state. Most of the political parties stand organized around the leaders. To cite an example, political parties like congress has two important personalities Ms Sonia Gandhi and Rahul Gandhi and at State level- GhulamNabi Azad and Saif-ud-din Soz. Similarly, National Conference stands for Farooq Abdullah and Omar Abdullah; PDP stand for Mufti Mohammad sayeed and Ms Mehbooba Mufti; Panthers Party is known by Prof. Bhim Singh, Harsh Dev Singh etc.

5. **Internal Factionalism:** Internal factionalism and groupings are also important features of the party system in the state politics. Sometime, the social relationship has also remained the cause of internal factionalism e.g. N.C observed the party-split when Sheikh Mohammad Abdullah nominated Dr. Farooq Abdullah as the president of the all Jammu and Kashmir National Conference at Hazratbal in 1982 ignorning his eldest son-in-law Ghulam Mohd. Shah NC government under the leadership of Farooq Abdullah was witnessed of factionalism by its other members when GM. Shah with his supports formed the government. He formed Awami National Confernce.

6. **No Strong Opposition:** Jammu and Kashmir National Conference played a dominant role in the state politics so there emerged no strong opposition. In its initial stage, Praja Parishad under the presidentship of Pt. Prem Nath Dogra was the only opposition of few members. It was not so effective.

   During NC-Cong I coalition government of 2008-2014, BJP, PDP, Panthers Party etc were the opposition parties. In PDP-BJP coal ition government 2015, congress I, NC and Panthers Party acted as opposition parties.

7. **Power Sharing with Central Government:** The Indian political system has developed a process of power-sharing with the regional political parties. Jammu and Kashmir National Conference and People's Democratic Party have remained the share-holders of power with the central Government. Omar Abdullah become the younest-minister during the 12th Lok Sabha Election at Central Government. He was a member of both the committee on Transport and Tourism and the ministry of Tourism's Consultative Committee. During 13th Lok Sabha Elections, he became the Union Minister of State, Commerce and Industry. He also enjoyed the portfolio of Union Minister of State for External Affairs as the younest- Union Minister.

Dr. Farooq Abdullah from NC also joined the UFA Government as a cabinet Minister. During 15th Lok Sabha Election, he became the Union Cabinet Minister for New and Renewable Energy.

Coalition Politics in Jammu and Kashmir State

Coalition politics is a system of governance by a group of political parties. It happens when no single political party gets a majority in the election to. form a government because people are not satisfied with the single majority rule and its failure leads towards coalition politics.

Roger Scruton defines coalition as a "political alliance of distinct parties or persons who preserve their political identities".

In the opinion of Ogg, "A coalition government is a collaborative or cooperative effort in which several political parties or some political parties in association with some independent representatives form a government".

Reasons Responsible for the Emergence of Coalition Politics in India

Congress party itself is responsible for the rise of coalition politics in India. The coalition has broken its monopoly over politics.

1. Political instability and crisis within political parties and confusion among the voters are responsible for the emergence of coalition politics.
2. Fundamental change in the structure of the society is also one of the important reasons for its emergence because the needs and interests of the masses are different from region to region in terms of class, religious, economic factors etc. Thus, it is not possible for a single political party to fulfill the different needs of the people.
3. Political defections are also responsible for its emergence. Few politicians of 'Aya Ram, Gaya Ram' nature are responsible for the making and unmaking of coalitions and for their failure also.
4. The opportunist politicians are also responsible for its emergence. They always watch their selfish interests. Coalition politics is the result of selfish and power hunger politicians.
5. National political parties neglect the regional interests. This results in the rapid growth of regional parties. These regional political parties represent the interests of the particular section. Each section prefers to choose its own representative rather than a party which promotes larger national interests. The verdict of the people, then, gives rise the formation of a coalition.

Nature of the Coalition Politics in India

1. Coalition politics is a joint effort of some political parties to secure the political power and form the government.
2. A coalition government is organised by more than two political parties.

3. When no single political party is in a position to get a 2/3 majority in the elections, some parties form a coalition after the poll verdict and form a government. This is known-as post-poll alliance.
4. In every coalition government, the coalition partners have share in the cabinet.
5. Some political parties have an alliance before election i.e. known as pre-poll alliance e.g. United Progressive Alliance, National Democratic Alliance.
6. These alliances have common party manifesto.
7. Sometimes, a few political parties form a coalition group or an alliance or a united front to restrict a particular political party or group from getting the chance to form a government, e.g. two United Fronts were formed in 1996-97 and 1997-98 in order to keep away the B.J.P. from forming a government. It was the negative nature of coalition politics.
8. Sometimes, the coalition group or alliance selects a common leader in advance or after the elections. The coalition government is organised under the leadership of such a person.
9. Coalition government is based upon a compromise or agreement.
10. A number of elected representatives of coalition partners have to be accommodated in the cabinet. Thus, a large sized council of ministers can be found in the coalition government, e.g. the NDA government had 74 ministers in the Council of Ministers.

Era of Coalition Politics in J&K State

The era of coalition politics in Jammu and Kashmir began in 1986 with Rajiv Farooq Accord. It was a pre-election alliance. The negotiations in this accord established the NC (F) and Congress (1) coalition Ministry in the state under the leadership of Dr. Farooq Abdullah.

The following were some agreed terms of Rajiv-Farooq Accord of 1986 which indicated the formation of coalition politics in a different nature—

- Both political parties had common ideology based on secularism, socialism, democracy and unity and integrity of India. Thus, both parties would support and cooperate each other and avoid wasting of their energies in fighting with each other.
- Both parties would cooperate each other against secessionist, communist and extremist-forces on political fronts.

- Both would work for rapid economic development of the state ***mu*** the betterment of its people at large.

This accord clear cut indicated the formation of coalition government. It was already decided that certain seats in the valley would be left for the congress candidates in 1987 elections and NC would support these candidates during elections.

State Legislative Assembly Election 2002 ·

During Assembly Election 2002, NC emerged as a single largest party with 28 seats but not willing to form the government. Then, it was a post-alliance between PDP and Congress I to form a coalition government. It was power-sharing politics between the two parties for a period of three years each. PDP under the leadership of Mufti Mohd-Sayeed decided to run the govt, for first three years so Congress candidate Pt. Mangat Ram Sharma became the Deputy C.M of the state. On 2nd November 2005, the Congress candidate Ghulam Nabi Azad joined the C.M. office for the remaining three years and PDP candidate Muzaffar Baig Became the Deputy C.M. of the state. But on 3rd September 2006, Baig formally resigned as Deputy CM. This coalition government was collapsed when the PDP withdrew from the INC-led state government in protest at the Amarnath land transfer decision. On 7th July 2008, Ghulam Nabi Azad resigned without facing a confidence of vote on the floor of the Assembly following withdrawal of support by PDP.

Summery of the J&K Assembly Elections Results of 2002, 2008 and 2014

Parry	Seats	Year		
		2002	**2008**	**2014**
1.	National Conference	28	28	15
2.	People's Democratic Party	16	21	28
3.	Indian National Congress	20	17	12
4.	Bhartiya Janta Party	01	11	25
5.	J&K People's Conference	0	0	0
6.	Communist Party of India (M)	2	1	1
7.	J&K People's Democratic Front	0	0	0
8.	J&K National Panthers Party	.4	3	0
9.	Bahujan Samaj Party	1	0	0
10.	J&K Democratic Party National ist	0	1	0
11.	People's Democratic Front	0	1	1
12.	Independents	15	11	4
		87		

State Lcgilative Assembly Elections 2008

During J&K Legislative Election 2008, NC emerged as a single largest party having 28 seats Congress debated to form a coalition government cither with NC or PDP, then, P.M. Manmohan Singh and Congress chairperson Ms Sonia Gandhi favoured the largest party to "honour the mandate" of the election. Thus, a coalition government was formed by NC and Congress in which Umar Abdullah sworn in as new and young CM. of J&K state for its full tenure.

State Legislative Assembly Election 2014

During 2014 Assembly elections, PDP was the single largest party with 28 seats and BJP became the second largest party with 25 seats. This election was recorded one of the highest voter turnouts in J&K state. In the politics of J&K state, for the first time, coalition government was formed with PDP-BJP alliance which was recognised as the meeting of "North Pole and South Pole" by the CM. Mufti Mohd. Sayeed. B.J.P candidate Dr. Nirmal Kumar Singh sworn in as the Deputy Chief Minister of the state. Inspite of Syeed, PDP's 13 and BJP's 11 MLAs took Oath as Ministers. Separatist turned politician Sajjad Gani Lone, Who met P.M. Modi ahead of the elections in Delhi, was also sworn-in as Science and Technology and Animal Husbandry Minister.

Unfortunately, after the sudden death of CM. Mufti Mohd. Sayeed on 7th January 2016, the Governor's Rule was imposed in the state on 8th January 2016 due to the constitutional crisis.

Ms. Mehbooba Mufti has become the first women Chief Minister of the Jammu & Kashmir state after the death of her father on 4th April, 2016.

Hence, the modern process of the democracy is better than the Amercian, and British democracy. It is important issue related with the author Dr. Shabnam Grewal as life long partner, as "In the beginning a God, and God was Holy Quran or Holy Ghost"=Rab.

Chapter - 17

Politics of Resettlement for Displacement People AFTER 1947 New History (Jammu & Kashmir A Victim)

A private member belonging to the ruling National Conference, Abdul Rahim Rather introduced the Resettlement Bill in the Legislative Assembly in March, 1980. The Purpose of the Bill was to legalise the return of all those persons who were class I and Class II state subjects before 14th May, 1954, but had migrated to the territory now included in Pakistan after 1st March, 1947 or for widows wives or descendants of such state subjects as desired to come back and resettle permanently in the state. For this purpose applications for such permits (As the State Government was authorized to issue under law) can confirm the concerned persons directly or through their relations living on this side (India) of the border. The Bill was also based on humanitarian considerations that it sought reunion of hard-pressed blood relations who were separated by the crucial circumstances of 1947. After its introduction, it was referred to a Select Committee in 1981. The Select Committee reported the bill back to the House. The Bill was passed by the state legislative and sent to the Governor for his assent.

The politics of Resettlement Bill became the hot discussion as between May 1982 to July 1987 between Centre & state government. The central government was of the opinion that the Bill would open flood gates to the spies to settle in the state. Sheikh Mohammad Abdullah met Indira Gandhi and tried to resolve the tensions. But the doubts on the Bill made the situation the worst. In these circumstances, the Governor referred the Bill to the Attorney General of India for legal opinion and after receiving the same, sent it back to the Legislature for reconsideration on the ground that it suffered from certain deficiencies.

- How all those persons who had deliberately and voluntarily migrated to Pakistan, settled there, taken Pakistani citizenship, appropriated evacuee property, served in the civil and armed services of Pakistan, fought against India or committed other treasonable acts against the country, can return to India or Kashmir as a matter of legal right?

- Even the wives, widows or descendants of the migrants born or to be born in Pakistan and having never been Indian citizens or never been State Subjects, would not be entitled to a legal right to come and settle in the state.
- Since the returnee had only to satisfy the competent authority regarding his intension to live permanently in the state, there was no provision or method to keep him forcibly in the state so that he could not go back to Pakistan or migrate elsewhere after he had sold his original property (evacuee property) or received such compensation in lieu thereof as he might be entitled to from the state.
- In the absence of any provision in the Bill for checking the antecedents of an applicant to satisfy the competent authority that he was not likely to be security risk, it opened the way for spices, saboteurs and foreign agents to settle in the state as a matter of legal right.
- Any persons who at any time chooses voluntarily to accept foreign nationality including Pakistan nationality looses the right to citizenship under articles 5, 6, 7, 8 and 9 of the Indian Constitution.
- Since it is the central government alone which controls the entry of foreigners into India, the state Legislature was not, therefore, competent to enact a Bill providing for the return from Pakistan of those persons who desired to come; back and resettle in the state. Hence, section 6 of the state constitution and the provision 2 to Article 7 as applicable to| J&K don't permit jurisdiction to the Bill under entries 17 and 19 of the Union List dealing with problems of admission into and explusion from India, passport and visas and citizenship, naturalization and aliens respectively.

The main criticism levelled against the Resettlement Bill introduced and passed by the State Legislature have been summarized in the following ways:-

- The bill was bound to involve the practical implications for the state's security and solidarity called lord Mount batten Plan of 1947.

- To secure the release of Azad-Kashmir from Pakistan so as to enable the people living in that territory to participate in the elections to the State Legislative for which 25 seats having already been kept reserved in the constitution of J&K and in the governance of the state.
- The Bill was bound to communalise the politics in the state resulting in weakening of its secular traditions, secular forces and secular basis.

The provision of the state constitution stand for constitutional recognition to the return of permanent residents form so called Azad Kashmir (POK) to their own native state i.e. J&K state. This recognition has not been accepted by the Government of India.

The Bill was taken up of re-consideration by the Legislative Assembly on sept. 25, 1982 and after a heated debate repassed on Oct, 4 1982 in its original form.

In less than one week after the Constitutional Bench returned the reference unanswered, the J&K National Panthers Party filed Writ Petition (Civil) No. 578/2001 in the Supreme Court Challenging the constitutionality of the Act. At the stage of mentioning of the writ Petition for its listing the operation of the Re-settlement Act was stayed. On 11th Nov. 2002, a three-judge Bench of the Court admitted the Writ petition and issued Rule and directed the order of stay to continue in operation. Writ Petition (civil) No. 578/2001, is still pending consideration. The final word has still to be said on the constitutional validity of the Act.

Note:- Dalit history is a part of the Constitutional history or law in the form of Dogra regiment of State CM Dhiyan Singh and Suchet Singh, in the previous life as Dalit rules of this state = Barwala Community (untouchables).

(Daya Sagar)

Chapter - 18

Ladakh Region: Demands and Politics with Special Reference to Hill Council of Sudra Concept as Elevated Race

The word Ladakh has been derived from La-taqs in Tibetan which literally means the '*Land of Mountain Passes*'. Ladakh lies in the northern most part of India which constitutes the two-third of total land mass of Jammu and Kashmir state. Ladakh has been known by different names at different time to cite an example Janet Rizvi described it as "*Cross Roads of High Asia*." Ladakh has two districts-Leh and Kargil, consisting of high peaks from 17000 to 20000 feet and above = Sodara Sufi Scholar (Dr. Raj-Rishi).

Leh is linked with the Kashmir Valley by the Zojila Pass (11,50,0ft) and forms part of the outer Himalayas. The district Leh is bounded by the International Border or Line of Control (LOC) with China in the North and East, and with Pakistan (POK) in the North.

Kargil town is located at a distance of 200 kms from Srinagar almost midway on the Srinagar - Leh National Highway, Kargil lies at an altitude ranging from 8000 ft to 14,000 ft above the sea level. Majority of its population is Muslims of Shia sect with a small amount of the Buddhists called as "Sarif log" of this areas.

(A) Ladakh: Historical Overview: During ancient period of human civilization, the present Ladakh was a part of Greater Ladakh spread over from Kailash Mansarover to Swaat (Dardistan). It is not available in the recorded history except references in the history of Kashmir, China, Mongolia, Kazakhistan and "Arab".

The great religions of the world— Buddhism, Islam and Christianity— reached Ladakh through missionaries in a very peaceful manner. There are two schools of Buddhist thought. First school of thought believes that Buddhism is originally introduced into Ladakh from Kashmir during the rule of Emperor Ashoka -the Great in third century B.C. The second school of thought is of the opinion that the Buddhism has entered into Ladakh during Kahishka's rule in second century A.D.

So far as Islam is concerned, it has been brought by Mir Ali Hamdani in around 1394 A.D. in Ladakh. Later on, a disciple of Syeed Ali Hamdani, Syeed Mohammad Norbaksh who visited Purig and Baltistan, rapidly converted the Baltis to Islam in scientific history of Dalit Muslims.

(B) Ladakh is Political History: ***The Political history of Ladakh—*** as an independent kingdom— begins with the setting up of a Tibetan dynasty in 950 A.D. The origin of the Ladakhi Kingdom is connected with the fall of the Tibetan monarchy in 842 A.D. With the assassination of "*Lang Darma*", a Central Tibetan Ruler, in 842 A.D., the long lineage of Tibetan kings came to an end. After the collapse of the Tibetan dynasty, the great grandson of Lang Darma, Skilde Nyima - Gon left Central Tibet about the year 900 A.D. and made his way towards Western Tibet in search of new dominions. He was said to have established his rule, probably in the provinces immediately to the East of present day Ladakh. Later on, he divided the region of Maryul comprising Guge, Purang and Zanskar between his three sons. His eldest son Spalgyigon (about 930-960 A.D) became the first king of Ladakh. His kingdom spread form Rudok in the East to Zojila in the West. However, it was only during 15th and 16th century that Ladakh - as an independent kingdom -gained political status when Namgayal dynasty came into power. This dynasty came to an end in 1842 when a Dogra General Zorawar Singh annexed Ladakh into the Dogra empire of Jammu (Dr. P.S. Jina).

Ladakh: Under Dogra Dynasty Till Independence and Accession

Ladakh was the celebrated Silk Route of China. It was a flourishing trade route across the Karokoram Pass to China, Lhasa, Yarkand and other cities of Central Asia. In 1834, Ladakh was attacked by Maharaja Gulab Singh, the Dogra Maharaja of Jammu, whose main motive was to gain possession of the profitable trade in Pashm-(Pashm means unprocessed raw-wool, whereas Pashmina is the cloth woven form Pashm)— Ladakh's only product of value. This invasion was led by the Dogra General Zorawar Singh Lord Dalhousic (1848-56). This invasion ended the existence of Ladakh as an independent kingdom. By the Treaty of Amritsar in 1846, the British handed over Kashmir to Majaraja Gulab Singh and Ladakh became a part of the new state of Jammu and Kashmir. Ladakh began to be ruled from Jammu through a Darbar Officer known as. Wazir-i-Wazarat appointed by the Maharaja. From 1870 under the Commercial Treaty concluded between the British and the Maharaja of Jammu and Kashmir, a British Official known as the British Joint Commissioner was posted at Leh during the summer to keep an eye watch in the matters connected with the Central Asia Trade. This treaty reflected the basic aim of the invasion as to gain control over the profitable trade in Pashm. Thus, Ladakh's relation with the Jammu and Kashmir Darbar was just that of an annexed kingdom or colony to its colonizer. The history of Dogra period is full of a number of examples of harassment, maltreatment and victimization of people by the officials. With the partition of India and signing of Instrument of Accession of Jammu and Kashmir, Ladakh became an integral part of India.

Ladakh Region: Demands and Politics

Demands of Ladakh region and its politics can be understood through the following headings:—

(1) Ladakh's Young Men Buddhist Association
(2) Ladakh Buddhist Association (LBA): Demand for Self-Rule
(3) Impact of Land Reform in Ladakh and role of National Conference
(4) Kushok Bakula: A voice for Ladakh's Autonomy
(5) Ladakh and Role of G.M Sadiq
(6) Division of Congress in Ladakh and Commercial Violence
(7) Demand for Scheduled Tribe Status.
(8) Ladakh: Scheduled Tribe Status.
(9) Violent Agitation in Ladakh: Demand for "Free Ladakh from Kashmir".
(10) Interference of Central Government and B.J.P. in Ladakh.
(11) Internal Discussions for Hill Council.
(12) Ladakh Autonomous Hill Development Council Act.

(1) Ladakh's Young Men Buddhist Association (YMBA) and Role of Sheikh Mohammad Abdullah: Right from 1947, Ladakhis had been demanding one form of the Central Rule or other. YMBA made its stand clear on behalf of Ladakh. This association gave two proposals through the memorandum — one to either join the neighbouring state of East Punjab or two, to be directly governed by the Centre. Ladakh was a part of the Kashmir region constitutionally and administratively but geographically and culturally, it was a poll part.

There was no serious effort made to accept Ladakh as equal partner in the decision-making process of the state inspite ofthe fact that Ladakh constituted 62.24% of the territory of Jammu and Kashmir. It was reflected from the fact that Sheikh Mohammad Abdullah's five member cabinet had only one representative from Jammu and none from Ladakh.

Sheikh Mohammad Abdullah was interested to empower the majority community of Kashmiri Muslims. In Ladakh, the Buddhists had been in maj ority and the Muslims were in maj ority. Thus, Muslim majority in the overall politics of the state occupied more space in the administration and economy of Ladakh. Due to this attitude, the Ladakhis felt neglected and marginalized and began to think in the terms of central Administration for the region.

(2) Ladakh Buddhist Association (LBA): Demand for Self-Rule: The president of Ladakh Buddhist Association (ŁBA) - Chhewang Rigzin - submitted a memorandum to Prime-Minister of India Pt. Jawahar Lal Nehru in May 1949 which demanded for self-rule. In July 1949, Pt. Nehru visited Ladakh alongwith Sheikh Abdullah and picked up Kushok Bakula to represent Ladakh to make befood the Pahari people = Animal culture. Bakula represented Ladakh in the State Legislative Assembly for a decade and half and dominated the political scene of Ladakh. He was considered as light of hope for Ladakhis.

(3) Impact of Land Reforms in Ladakh and role of National Conference: Under the revolutionary programme of land reforms in the state, the National conference transferred 8,00,000 acres of land to 2,47,000 tillers without any compensation to the owners. It was criticized on communal grounds because mostly landlords in Jammu and Ladakh were Hindus and Buddhists. The land was the major property of the monasteries in Ladakh. The land reform was considered as an attack on the Buddhist clergy. Ladakhis were worried about to protect their religion and culture. The Gompas (Buddhist Temples) received no financial aid under various projects of the state government. The government showed indifferent attitude while transferring Zanskar (a Buddhist dominant area in Kargil district) to Leh tehsil. Moreover, people showed resentment for the implementation of Urdu in Ladakh schools. The scholarships for children of backward areas and grant-in-aid provided under the Dogra rule for three primary schools run by Shias, Sunnis and Buddhists had been disconnected by the government. It was an unfortunate part that no allocation was made in the first budget for Ladakh's development.

(4) Kushok Bakula: A voice for Ladakh's Autonomy: Kushok Bakula— as the first M.LA from Ladakh and later as the Deputy Minister— raised voice from time to time for Ladakh's autonomy. Politically, Kashmiri leaders had blocked autonomy for the regions within the state. The Ladakhi leaders alleged that the Kashmiri rulers had always indulged in discriminating.

(5) Ladakh and Role of G.M Sadiq: During the Sino-Indian War of 1962, a demand for the introduction of central administration along the lines of North East Frontier Agency (NEFA) was raised because Ladakh came under central adminitrtion for a brief period. But this was withdrawn soon after G.M. Sadiq took over the reigns of power in 1964. Ladakhis started a resistance movement. The Congress party under Kushok Bakula started agitation for the restoration of direct central administration in Ladakh. In order to suppress this movement, Chief-Minister G.M. Sadiq encouraged a new leadership of Lamas by favouring Kushok Thiksay over Kushok Bakula. On the other hand, he favoured the Muslim leadership of Kargil over the Buddhist leadership of Leh! It gave birth to communalism in Ladakh.

(6) Division of Congress in Ladakh and Commercial Violence: In 1967, the Indian National Congress was divided into Congress A and Congress B in Ladakh. Congress - A was headed by Kushok Bakula and Congress- B was headed by Kushok Thiksay. Muslims and some other leaders joined Congress -B. Communal violence took place in June 1969. The political division of Congress created bitter feelings among the Buddhists themselves. The agitation weakened when Bakula Rinpoche and his close associate Sonam Wangail accepted minor concession from G.M. Sadiq government.

(7) Demand for Scheduled Tribe Status: The Buddhist Action Committee raised their demand for Scheduled Tribe Status in which it demanded:—

- Settlement of the Tibetan refugees in Ladakh
- Making of the Bodhi language as compulsory subject upto high school.
- Ladakh's political representative be a full-fledged cabinet minister.

These demands were rejected by the state government on account of strong opposition from the Muslim Action Committee. As a result, the Muslim of Kargil - who are predominantly Shia— began to see their interests closely linked to those of Kashmiri, which shared nothing but religion.

(8) Ladakh: Scheduled Tribe Status: The Ladakhis region was declared as Scheduled Tribe Area by confering Scheduled Tribe Status on eight ethnic tribes of Ladakh on Oct 7, 1989.

(9) Violent Agitation in Ladakh: Demand for "*Free Ladakh from Kashmir*": The Ladakh Buddhist association launched a violent agitation in October, 1989. It gave the call for "*Free Ladakh from Kashmir,*" and demanded Union Territory Status. Three persons died and several seriously injured during this agitation. LBA gave a call for socio-economic boycott of Muslim because the trade and tourism were controlled by the people from the Kashmir Valley.

(10) Interference of Central Government and B.J.P in Ladakh: The Prime Minister Rajeev Gandhi proposed autonomous Hill Council for Ladakh against the wishes of the then state's Chief-Minister Dr. Farroq Abdullah. A tri-partite agreement among the Government of India, of the state and the LBA was signed at Leh on October 29, 1989 under which Leh was to get an Autonomous Hill Council. Hence, LBA suspended its demand for Union Territory Status in the favour of an Autonomous Hill Council and called off the agitation. This agreement suffered a serious set-back as the Congress I was out of power at the centre.

Meanwhile the boycott with Muslims continued in Ladakh for three years till 1992 when the Central Government interfered to persuade the LBA to lift the boycott. The LBA developed a close relationship with the Hindu nationalist forces in order to win central sympathy for its demands. As a result, the Bhartiya Janta Party (B.J.P) repeatedly wrote to the then Prime-Minister. P.V. Narasimha Rao about Ladakhi concerns in parliament. The Buddhists also agreed to patch up with the Muslims and took the support of the Ladakh Muslim Association (LMA). The Muslims co-operated with the Buddhists in their struggle co-operated with the Buddhists in their struggle for greater autonomy known as Hill Council Status.

(11) Internal Discussions for Hill Council: On June 10-11, 1993, the representatives of LBA and the LMA held discussions in Srinagar with state government officials on the structures and constitution of the council. The Chief Secretary Sheikh Ghulam Rasool represented the state Government whereas Thupstan Chhewang represented the LBA and Akbar Ladakhi— the LMA. Various points of disagreement were resolved by the Central Government. Consequently, on October 9, 1993, the government finally allowed to form an autonomous Hill Council for Leh and Kargil as well.

(12)Ladakh Autonomous Hill Development Council Act: On My 9,1995 through a Presidential order theLadakh Autonomous Hill Development Council Act was enacted during the regime of Prime-Minister. P.V Narsimha Rao. It provided an Autonomous Hill Council each for Leh and Kargil, and an Inter-District Council to advise them on the matters of common interest. Later on, the Act was passed by the State Assembly on October 3,1997 known as Ladakh Autonomous Hill Development Council Act, 1997.

Note:- Ladakh is wonderful land of India, it is now growing a strong tourist spot for the foreigners and the Indian; during the time of summer, looking like as tiny Japan in the modern world and more than that. (Dr. Raj Rishi ke Statement: "History of Chamar Dynasty" : p. 8).

Chapter - 19

Regional Demand and Politics = Idea of Development in History (1947 to 2017)

And Study the Book of Miss Ramiyan Bhardwaj ("Studies in Kashmir Politics = Brahminmat"

I

Jammu and Kashmir state is a state of three geographically dislocated after 1947, multi-culturally, multi linguistic and multi racial, regional & sub-regional cultures, religious regions i.e. Jammu, Kashmir and Ladakh. These three regions have political and emotional differences also. Its geo-political profile has heterogeneous in nature. Thus, the feeling of regionalism has been deeply rooted in the state like Kashmir region as world level. J&K State is multi linguistic, multi cultural, racial and ethnical state .It consists of three regions- Jammu, the Kashmir valley and Ladakh. These regions have different regional and political personalities.

By the treaty of Amritsar with the British Govt, in 1846, Maharaja Gulab Singh was succeeded to make this state a distinct political entity. In the initial years of the Dogra Rule in the state, most of the offices were held by the outsiders. After acquiring the important governmental posts in the state, they also invited their relatives in the state. Their relatives also secured minor posts. The people of the state "particularly Muslims were not educated so the injustice could not be felt. After the establishment of the two Degree Colleges— one in Jammu (Prince of Wales College, now, called G.G.M. Science College) and other in Srinagar (Amar Singh College) and spread of Western Education, the Muslims became conscious for the governmental job and raised issues against the outsiders. Thus, a movement Kashmir for Kashmiris began in valley during the period of Maharaja Pratap Singh. The inter-regional demands had been remained continued even after independence called Azadi. Destructive Approach of the Separatists of India.

Jammu Vs Kashmir : Inter Regional Demand And Politics

Jammu & Kashmir is a pluralist society in the sense that it has social and political diversities. So far as Jammu region is concerned, it is the most heterogeneous division in the context of the religious, linguistic, cultural, tribal and caste categories of the state. Jammu region has the Hindu population but the Muslims have a strong presence over there.

Jammu region is a political reality beyond the Kashmir Valley. While focusing on Jammu, a difference can be seen between the Kashmir Valley and the J&K State as a whole. The state is beyond the Kashmir Valley. It has two more regions i.e. Jammu and Ladakh which are culturally and politically different from Kashmir.

Jammu is culturally diverse. The region reflects a multi-religious, multi-cultures and multi-linguistic society. Though it is Hindu-majority region but it has also a number of Gujjar-Muslims. There are 10 districts of Jammu region. Muslim population is very low in Jammu, Samba and Kathua districts. Another 4 districts - Poonch, Rajouri, Doda and Kishtwar are having Muslims majority and there is very thin minority of Hindus of Jammu region. The rest ofthe three districts of Reasi, Udhampur and Ramban have a large number of Hindus with sizeable number of Muslims.

Inspite of Hindus and Muslims, Gujjars alongwith Bakerwals and Gaddis have their own different identity in this region. Basically, Gujjars are nomadic but most of them are in the process of settling down. Gujjars and Bakerwals are Muslims but Gaddis are Hindus. They prefer to identify themselves by their tribes and not by religious identity. They are particularly resided in the two border districts of Poonch and Rajouri. There are Paharis located in the districts of Doda, Kishtwar and Ramban.

The Nature Of Politics In Jammu = CASTE BASED STUDY.

It was only 1846 that the state was formed as one unit consisted of three regions- Jammu, Kashmir and Ladakh. Before 1846, there was no interaction between the two religions. It was only through the Dogra rulers who exercised his powers over the state that some common linkage was established.

During 2nd and 3rd decade of the 20th century, politics became a medium for establishing linkage between the regions of Jammu and Kashmir. The political awakening took place in Kashmir against the Dogra ruler. The formation of All J&K Muslim Conference was a combined response of both Jammu and Kashmir regions. Muslim Conference had very prominent leaders from both regions i.e. S.M. Abdullah from Kashmir and Choudhary Abbas & Allah Rakha from Jammu. But after the conversion of Muslim Conference into National Conference in 1939, it reflected the difference between the leadership of Kashmir and Jammu. Hence, the Jammu-based leaders revived the Muslim Conference.

The split of the Muslim politics of the state on the regional basis became the cause of the regionalization of the Kashmiri Identity Politics. National Conference leaders did not concentrate on the Jammu region. As a result, here developed the political polarization between two regions before the instrument of accession. A number of agitations were taken place in Jammu region after the accession. The land reforms was the major reason for resentment among the propertied classes. Land was transferred to the landless peasantry mostly belonging to the lower castes which were estimated to be around two lakhs and fifty thousand in the Jammu province. Both Hindu and Muslims landowners of Jammu region were not happy for these reforms. Moreover, the Jammu and Kashmir Government was not in the favour of compensations while acquiring the land beyond the payment of ceiling limit.

Contestation of the Kashmiri's politics, especially its emphasis on autonomy, became the hallmark of Jammu's politics in the immediate post-accession period. In 1952, a sustained agitation against Article370 was launched by Praja Parishad with demand for the abolition of Article 370 and full constitutional integration of the state with India.

1. Agitation of 1952 by Praja Parishad

Praja Parishad Launched an agitation in 1952 with the slogan "*Ek Vidhan, Ek Pradhan, EkNishan and One Nation. One tax as GST. Study*". It became popular in Jammu region because it articulated the local resentment against the indifference of Kashmir based National Conference Government to concerns of people of Jammu. The Praja Parishad raised the issue of bias of the state government vs. Jammu region in various matters including land-reforms, custom barriers between state and India, issue of rehabilitation of refugees and ex-servicemen and lack of employment opportunities for the people of the Jammu region.

Jammu region was discriminated in the matters of political power sharing, appointments, promotion, admission to professional institution. A feeling of regional negligiance was emerged. Regional negligiance encouraged various agitations in this region on the issues like regional development, employment in the state services, admission to professional and other educational institutions, the distribution of resources between the two regions, establishment of educational or other institutions or even decisions to shift the annual office move from Jammu. Amongst these agitations, two agitation-the Jammu Autonomy Forum and the Poonch Agitation had the most significant role.

(i) Jammu Autonomy Forum : 1966-67

A movement to promote the Jammu cause was engineered during 1966-67. It was launched by the political groups of Anant Ram Shastri's Dogra Mandal (DM) and Balraj Puri's Jammu Autonomy Forum. Dogra Mandal demanded for Jammu's separation, from Kashmir and its merge with Himachal Pradesh (H.P) whereas the JAF's battle-cry was constitutional guarantees of regional rights. The most significant aspect of the political situation in Jammu was the participation in the movement of the entire student community, which had been filled with anger by the government's decision to close down the Jammu Ayurvedic College (MLA Shyam Lal ke Dukan).

Meanwhile the State Government appointed Gajendra Gadkar Commission (See Appendix 11 for more details) to look into the complaints of the people and regional imbalances.

(ii) Poonch Agitation: October 1978

97 days' movement was launched by the rejected qualified candidates against the backdoor appointment of teachers by the District Recruitment Board Poonch in Oct 1978.

Again in order to find out the grievances of the people of the three regions, the Sikri Commission (See appendix XII) was set up by the State Government.

But the State Government took no action on these and several other recommendations to harmonize inter-regional relations. Meanwhile, Kashmir sought to discontinue the 130 year-old practice of moving the secretariat from Jammu to Srinagar and back and set it up permanently in Srinagar in 1987. The move failed to face the strong opposition from Jammu.

Demand for Regional Autonomy for Jammu

Almost all political parties and organizations raised the demand for Regional Autonomy for the Jammu during the period of militancy. They demanded for regional councils for Jammu & Ladakh. This demand was so vocal that National Conference acknowledged it during State Assembly

Elections 1996 and committed itself to make a provision for regional autonomy if it returns to power. After forming the government, the N.C. established the Regional Autonomy Committee which recommended reorganization of Jammu into three different regions. It was negative in nature.

Jammu: Intra-regional Demands

During the period of militancy, the militancy spread in large barts of the Jammu region, especially in the Doda and Poonch-Rajouri belt. The dominant politics of these two regions revolved pund the developmental issues. Last 25 years, the political classes of these two areas have been vocal about the need for political and Iconomic empowerment of these areas. The following Intra-regional demands in Jammu have been articulated during the period of militancy only:-

1. Demand for Chenab Valley Hill Council
2. Demand for Pir Panchal Hill Council

1. Demand for Chenab Valley Hill Council: The Doda belt has backward and marginalized population as Chandals of the previous history of Ambedkar, now called themselves Brahmins or NC and Congress workers. It has underdevelopment. As the Hindu-majority area of Jammu region, the people blame the "Kashmir-Centric government for ignoring the interest of this area. The people of Doda belt feel that they are marginalized by both the Kashmir-based politics and Jammu-based regional elites. They have made the demand for Chenab Valley Hill Council on the pattern of Leh and Kargil Development Council so that they may solve their own issues.

2. Pir Panchal Hill Council: People of Poonch-Rajouri belt have been given importance to their own specific issues relating to their border. The nature of their political problems and struggles has been different from that of the Kashmiris. They have the feeling of 'Double Marginalisation' both at the hands of Kashmir-based government and Jammu-based regional elites. Such type of marginalization is reflected on demanding for Pir-Panchal Hills Council.

II

Ladakh Vs Kashmir Inter-regional Demands And Politics

Ladakh became an independent kingdom in 10th century after breaking up of the Tibetan empire. Ladakh was ruled by its own J kings near about

800 years. After the annexation of Ladakh by I Zorawar Singh in 1842, Ladakh remained a part of Dogra kingdom for the next century and Ladakh with the accession of Jammu & Kashmir to India, Ladakh became a part of Indian Union in 1947.

Ladakh was an overall backward region. It has its own geographical and political differences with Kashmir. It is a part of the Kashmir region constitutionally and administratively also. In Ladakh, the Buddhists have been in majority and Muslims are a substantive minority as Chamar by Caste. There was no Ladakhi representative in Sheikh Mohammad Abdullah's government, Sheikh Abdullah was also interested to empower the majority community of Kashmiri Muslims. Hence, the Muslim majority in the overall politics of state occupied more space in the administration and economy of Ladakh. Due to this attitude, the Ladakhis felt neglected and marginalized and began to think in terms of Central Administration for the region. Moreover, the Buddhists were disappointed with the land reforms in the Ladakh region which was considered as an attack on the Buddhist Clergy and "Chamar Preist". They raised the demand for separation from the Kashmir Valley as a separate status of Ladakh as Dalit region.

Valley leadership had systematically ignored Ladakh in all walks of life and that the State Government had not taken into consideration of their complaints and grievances of regional imbalance in the field of power generation, tourism development, education, industrial development etc. The state had discriminatory attitude towards the Ladakhis. In 1952, the Ladakhis under the inspiration of the Head Lama of Ladakh, Kushak Bakula demanded an effective say in the State Politics and administration. They also asserted that they would join Tibet in the event of the centre agreeing to Sheikh Mohammad Abdullah's demand for greater autonomy. However, in 1964, they launched an organized strugg'e against the "Kashmiri Domination" and demanded a "NEFA-type" Central Administration. Ladakh witnessed a communal problem when the Buddhists supported the demand for the settlement of Tibetan refugees in Ladakh district whereas the Muslim Action Committee opposed it as creating ethnic imbalances in the region. The Buddhists also had a fear of reduction to minority because there were a lot of incidents of conversion of the Buddhist girls to Islam on the encouragement of *Anjuman-i-Islam* which provides the Muslim youngmen money to attract the Buddhist girls to accept Islam as Falak Madam Bi. and Choudhary, Dr. Munior Hussain (Principal).

The people of this region developed a feeling of political negligence of the region by the Kashmir centric politics. This feeling of alienation and marginalization formed a religious association-Ladakh Buddhist Association (LBA). In its initial stages, it claimed to demand in the name of all Ladakhis but later on, religious based politics of Ladakh, soon, separated the Muslim community of Ladakh from LBA's politics. The Muslims of Ladakh formed their own political organization—the Ladakh Muslim Association (LMA). Its fonnation on religious basis resulted in the creation of Ladakh Muslim Identity in Ladakh.

Various movements began during 1974-1982 under the leadership of Lama Lobzang, Thupstan Chewang and P. Namgyal respectively demanding autonomy for Ladakh (Dr. P.S. Jina ke Kitab).

Gajendragadkar Commission and the Sikri Commission (See appendix XI & XII) acknowledged that Ladakh had no share in the state's political administration and economic set up. These commissions recommended a few measures much as setting up of a separate development board for Ladakh, including of atleast one Ladakhi in the State Cabinet, establishment of a Degree College & at Zanzkar, Nobra etc, stable and satisfactory arrangements for providing electricity etc. But the state government did not consider these concessions. It distributed the social equilibrium of Ladakh in 1979 by dividing it into Leh and Kargil districts on purely communal lines. The motive was to play the Muslim-majority Kargil against the Buddhist-majority Leh and weaken the autonomy movement. It was under these circumstances the LBA launched a violent struggle on 15th July, 1989 to achieve Union Territory Status for Ladakh. Meanwhile, the Ladakh region was declared as Scheduled Tribe Status on 8 ethnic tribes of Ladakh on 7th October, 1989 have been mentioned in the book of Dr. S.P. Vaid, "*Socio Economic Roots of Unrest in Jammu & Kashmir State*". The Ladakh Buddhist Association (LBA) launched a violent agitation which gave call for "*Free Ladakh from Kashmir*" and demanded Union Territory Status. It gave a call for socio-economic boycott of Muslim because the trade and tourism were controlled by the Kashmiri people.

This boycott continued for three year till 1992 and discontinued with the interference of the Central Government. The Buddhists agreed to patch up with the Muslims and took the support of Ladakh Muslim Association (LMA). Ladakh was bifurcated into two districts- Leh and Kargil. Later on, on October 3, 1997, Ladakh Autonomous Hill Development Council and Kargil Autonomous Hill Development Council were constituted by an act passed by the State Assembly known as Ladakh Autonomous Hill Development Council Act, 1997.

Ladakh : Intra-Regional Demands and Politics

In 2000, the Ladakh Buddhist Association again presented a memorandum to the members of Parliament justifying the renewal of its Union Territory Demand. By 2002, a political front i.e. Ladakh Union Territory Front was established aiming at dissolving all party and political differences to put forth a unified fight for UnionTerritory. It was supported by both the Buddhist and Muslim leaders of Leh. But later on, its shortcomings were exposed.

Union Territory movement remains only on a vote bank apparatus. All the political parties having their respective bases in Leh, procure votes in the name or with the pledge of acquiring Union Territory Status for Ladakh, and the leaders in Kargil purchase votes by opposing the same. Thus, every parliamentary election in Ladakh gets reduced to Union Territory and religious affairs, nothing more than a Leh-Buddhist vs Kargil-Muslims or supporters and non-supporters of Union Territory demand.

The Buddhist elites of Leh have again launched their demand for Union Territory Status. Religious associations have been playing a significant role in the politics of Ladakh. LBA and LMA are associated with outside forces which can prove very dangerous for the inter-community dynamics. LBA has a close relations with BJP and finds support in the rightist elements of Jammu region. In fact, they are jointly raising the demand of reorganization of the state and separation of their representative regions from Kashmir. LBA has openly been associating itself with VHP, RSS and Panun Kashmir movement of the landless people of India. These relations can be disturbed the communal harmonv of ladakh. On the other side, Kashmiri leaders support Kargil on the basis of religious identity to dissolve the demands of Ladakh. They try to provoke Muslim sentiments of Kargil against the Buddhist identity= weak successor of the Hindu status.

III
Kashmir : Intra Regional Demands And Politics

The demands and "*Politics*" or "*Ranjiti*" of Kashmir can be understood under the following headings:

1. Demand for Plebiscite and Formation of Plebiscite Front.
2. Awami Action Committee: Politics of Religion to Kashmir Issue.
3. Rajiv-Farooq Accord of 1986 vs Muslim United Front.
4. Rise of Militancy and Separatism: Popular Support.
5. Collapse of State Assembly in 1989: Governor Rule.

6. Formation of Hurriyat Conference.
7. Role of Surrendered Militants.
8. Changing Role of Women towards Militancy.
9. Migration of Kashmiri Pandits from Kashmir.
10. Separatist assertion from 2008-10.

1. Demand for Plebiscite and Formation of Plebiscite Front: Sheikh Mohammad Abdullah raised a demand for plebiscite that was the beginning of the separatist politics of Kashmir in 1953. For the fulfilment of this demand, a senior member of National Conference and a close friend of Sheikh Mohammad Abdullah, MirzaAfzal Beg formed Plebiscite Front in 1955. Whole Kashmiris especially rural masses completely involved in this demand. '*Raishumari*' became the catch phrase of Kashmir for the coming twenty years.

This demand was based on the participation of Jammu and Kashmir people to finalize the accession of the state with India as per the UN resolution (See appendix XIII). This front criticized the local government on number of issues of Kashmir relationship with India and other issues related to policy-making. Sheikh Abdullah and Beg kept themselves busy to engage the government on issues relating to making of constitution to Centre-State relations etc. The Plebiscite Front was considered as a symbol of people's opposition.

2. Awami Action Committee: Politics of Religion to Kashmir Issue: A religious incident (issue of disappearance of the Holy Relic from the Hazratbal Shrine) happened in Kashmir. Mass comminication participation got a platform to express themselves. The people were totally against Bakshi Gulam Mohammad. There emerged political reaction of the people and anti-government slogans. Under such circumstances, Maulana Masoodi and other important persons like Mirwaiz Maulvi Farooq and G.M. Karra formed Awami Action Committee. This committee played important role in the politics of Kashmir and demanded the resolution of Kashmir conflict. For the first time in the past accession period, a number of Kashmiri youth were mobilized and demanded for self-determination. Hence, the politics of separatism spread in the decade of 1960s, during the birth of Raj-Rishi of Kashmir in alive form.

3. Rajiv Farooq Accord of 1986 vs Muslim United Front: Rajiv-Farooq Accord of 1986 brought unrest in Kashmir and weakened National Conference in the Kashmir politics. Under such circumstances, Muslim United Front (MUF) was formed on religious basis. It encouraged the anti-

Congress and anti-Centre sentiments and aims at promotion and protection of Islamic solidarity, fundamental principles of Islam etc. In 1987 State Assembly Elections, MUF and People's Conference, together gave a very neck to neck fight to NC-Congress (I). After the formation of NC-Congress. After the formation of NC-Congtess aliance government, the political situation became worst because the opponents of the government were ruthlessly treated in Retentions. As a result, in 1988 many young men left their professional and educational studies incomplete and crossed the border to get training for militancy.

4. Rise of Militancy and Separatism: Popular Support: After the 1987 Assembly Elections, the armed militancy emerged in Kashmir which was strongly supported by the people of Kashmir. Sense of alienation and anger of the people were the main causes of its emergence. Various protest movements throughout the period between 1987 and 1989 provided the space for mobilization of the people. Kashmir Valley was swayed by the sentiments of 'Azadi'.

The Kashmiris gathered in thousands and demanded the implementation of UN Resolution on Kashmir issue. For it, they marched towards the office of UN Military Observers' Group (UNMOG).

The Militancy during this period flourished with the support of the Kashmiri masses. The militants were respected by them. They freely moved in the streets. Hence, the armed militancy was legitimized through the popular separatist sentiments.

5. Collapse of State Assembly in 1989 (Governor Rule): There was a breakdown of the Constitutional Machinery in the State so the state assembly was dissolved in January, 1990 due to the involvement of militancy in the state. As a result, the Governor rule was imposed on the State. Later on, it came under the President's rule till 1996.

6. Formation of Hurriyat Conference: In order to politicize the popular separatist sentiments and armed militancy, All Party Hurriyat Conference was formed under the chairmanship of Maulvi Omar Farooq. Hurriyat Conference included seven parties and twenty other groups and organizations. It included the Muslim Conference, Jamat-e-Islami, People's Conference, People's League, Awami Action Committee and JKLF. It has the following important objectives:-

(i) To struggle for exercise of rights of self-determination as per the UN Charter and as per the resolutions adopted by the UN Security Council.

(ii) To make efforts for alternative negotiated settlement of the dispute.

(iii) To project the movement at the international level.

(iv) To promote Islamic Values and preserve the Muslim-majority character of the State.

It occupied a central space in the separatist politics of Kashmir. It provided a political face to the separatism.

7. Role of Surrendered Militants: The people of Valley faced violence during early 1990's. It was only because of the presence of foreign militants. Thus, the surrendered militants began to work for the State and helped the State agencies to restore its authority in various space.

8. Changing Role **of Women Towards Militancy:** Women had also changed their ideas about militancy. They were victimized during militancy - sexually abused by the security forces as well as militants. Hence, they silently opposed it.

9. Migration of Kashmiri Pandits from Kashmir: There was no tension between the Kashmiri Pandits and Kashmiri Muslims befor 1986. Due to damage to some temples during public protests in Anantnag in 1986, it created communal tension among the Kashmiri Pandits. They became conscious of their minority status and felt isolated in the political activity for 'Azadi'. Moreover, the militants targeted the prominent Kashmiri Pandits including political leaders of BJP, judges etc. They were considered as Indian Agents and informers. On the other hand, there was a sympathetic policy of the state, particularly of J&K Governor Jagmohan, to send the Kashmiri Pandits away so that it might suppress the protestors by ruthless means as idiot Governor of the J&K State.

During this period, a number of militant organizations emerged which pressurized the Kashmiri Pandits to leave Kashmir. These organizations launched a terror campaign through letters, posters, pamphlets etc. These activities created a fear among the Kashmiri Pandits. As a result, they were compelled to leave the Kashmir Valley. Still, they have been residing in Jammu region and other parts. There is a question mark on their return to Kashmir.

10. Separatist Assertion from 2008-10: Kashmir involved in protest mass movements during 2007 on administrative issues like demand for new tehsils, colleges, human rights violation.

Kashmir was totally unrest during 2008 on the issues of an order of the State Government to divert 800 canals of forest land to Shree Amarnath

Shrine Board (SASB) for the purposes of erecting pre-fabricated temporary structures for housing the pilgrims during the period of annual Amarnath pilgrimage. The separatists used this issue to make fear among Kashmiri about 'demographic change'. They made the Kashmiris to believe the Indian policy for the entry of Non-Muslims in the State which could change the Muslim-Majority character of the state. The mass agitation in Kashmir compelled the government to withdraw the order. But its withdrawal gave birth to massive agitation in the Jammu region. There was a strong assertion of separatist sentiments during these two phases of agitation. The separatist leaders gave call to march to different places. They also protested against the human rights violation by security forces, rape and murder issues etc.

Inspite of the demand for self-determination, the slogan like 'Go India Go' & 'Quit Kashmir' were raised during 2010 as a religious flavor among peoples.

Progressive Idea In Kashmir Politics

For a long time in historical phenomena, "*politics*" has been regarded as a study of the State. According to Garner, "Politics begins with the state and ends up with the State" = Decline of British rule in India and rising of the local politics, as maturity base knowledge of India and Pakistan. Historical approach is one of the important approaches to the study of politics. It advocates the study of politics as history of the Jammu and Kashmir State is still exisiting in conflict due to lack of knowledge and understanding with Dalit rulers of Barnai Dera. (*Early History Of Jammu & Kashmir Region*). Southern Indian became demoralized, why because of the '*History Repeat Itself*' by the Dalit historian for "Postivism". "Negativism" which begins, after 1947, as First Prime Minister of India Pt. Jawaharlal Nehru before him, Mohan Das Karm Chand Gandhi initiated politics with "Dalit Christian" of England with dominance of Queen Proclamation of 1858 and ended with the growth of history, who were the Sudras? As Aryan

The big Hindus of South India, they were encouraged to participate in National Movement local politics as a progressive idea in history as RSS. But Hindu has 'no history' "Dalits hagve History".

Prime Minister Liaquat Ali Khan, talks on Kashmir issue = Kashmiri Islamic Ideology and society = one group + there was no understanding between the local parties and the Congress, that was at that times on the whelm of the affair, Sheikh Abdullah = Kisan Bisakhi Ram = illiterate farmer left the village ideology settled in Jammu region as an old man. He

(Bisakhi Ram) interviewed with the writer Miss Ramiyan Bhardwaj PM or CM of Kashmir, said in Delhi that Kashmir has acceded to the Indian Union because of economic need. Where stands the Instrument of Accession Hari Singh as incapable ruler of Jammu and Kashmir State in comparison with Dr. Raj-Rishi and Dr. Shabnam Grenail Gangotra. So far as economic relations are concerned, it is a backward state (India and Pakistan as two dominion). One was dominated by Muslims and other was dominated by Hindus, so called India Dalits, there were not aware of their basic rights at one time, now, they are aware the polities but unsucessful due to lack of majority. India informed Pakistan and other Dominion representatives = Dr. B.R. Ambedkar about the majority of Dalit India = backward nation + caste rigidity It had been decided to refer the "Kashmir Issue" to the security council under article 35 of the UN charter. With the passage of time India and Pakistan, emerged as strong states as of the other states like China and Japan. This event was took place in Nov. 30, 1947.

By analyzing the term *'History'* as story of God and Man, Quran says, "In the Name of Allah, the most Beneficent, the most Merciful", that is realizing soul God spirit of the positivism. And, along with many topics of the study which Holy Quran or Holy Words has to be discussed for the belief of Oneness Nam-History and politics. But from the capitalist democracy- that is inevitably narrow and stealithily pushes aside the poor section of the society, but engineer, doctors, they are well-up with corruption methods with the hypocrcy of politicians and corrupt clerks (AS) and there is no doubt, there is development from Pt. Jawahar Lal Nehru to Raj Rishi of Kashmir, but lacuna is there for the establishment of good governance. As there are liberal professors in JNU like Amit Mattoo and Vikram Harijan (Allahabad University), but in Jammu and Kashmir, there is less competence to move ahead to construction new India as Englisthan. (Lenin, the State Revolution; pp. 1-83)

APPENDICES

Appendix - I

Treaty of Lahore

Treaty between the British Government and the State of Lahore, concluded at Lahore on March 9th, 1846, as the study of "Kashmir Issue".

Whereas the treaty of amity and concord, which was concluded between the British Government and the late Maharaja Ranjit Singh, the ruler the Lahore in 1809, was broken by the unprovoked aggression on the British provinces-of the Sikh Army, in December last, and whereas, on that occasion, by the proclamation dated the 13th of December, the territories then in the occupation of the Maharaja of Lahore, on the left or British bank of the river Satluj, were confiscated and annexed to the British provinces; and since that time, hostile operations have been prosecuted by the two governments, the one against the other, which have resulted in the occupation of Lahore by the British troops. And whereas it has been determined that upon certain conditions, peace shall be re-established between the two Governments, the following treaty of peace between the Honourable English East India Company, the Maharaja Dalip Singh Bahadur, and his children, heir and successors, has been concluded on the part of the Honourable Company, by Frederick Currie, Esq, and Brevet-Major Henry Montgomery Lawrence, by virtue of full powers to that effect vested in them by the right Honourable Sir Henry Hardinge, G.C.B., one of Her Brittanic Majesty's most Honourable Privy Council, Governor-General appointed by the Honourable Company to direct and control all their affairs in the East-Indies, and on the part of his Highness the Maharaja, Dalip Singh, by Bhai Ram Singh, Raja Lai Singh, Sadar Tej Singh, Sardar Chattar Singh Attariwala, Sardar Ranjor Singh, Majithia, DiwanDinaNathand Fakir Nur-ud-din vested with full powers and authority on the part of his Highness.

Article 1

There shall be perpetual peace and friendship between the British Government, on the one part, and Maharaja Dalip Singh, his heirs and successors on the other.

Article 2

The Maharaja of Lahore renounces for himself, his heirs and successors all claim to or connection with, the territories lying to the South of the river Satluj, and engages never to have concerned with those territories or the inhabitants thereof.

Article 3

The Maharaja ceded to the Honourable Company in perpetual sovereignty, all his forts, territories, and rights in the Doab and country, hill and plain, situate between the rivers Beas and Satluj.

Article 4

The British Government having demanded from the Lahore State, and indemnification for the expenses of the war, in addition to the cession of territory described in Article 3, payment of a one and a half crores of rupees; and the Lahore Government being unable to pay the whole of this sum at this time, or to give security satisfactory to the British Government of its eventual payments; the Maharaja cedes to the Honourable Company, in perpetual sovereignty, as equivalent for one crore of rupees all his forts, territories, rights and interests in the hill countries which are situated between the river Beas and Indus, including the Provinces of Kashmir and Hazara.

Article 5

The Maharaja will pay to the British Government the sum of fifty lacs of rupees, on or before the ratification of this treaty.

Article 6

The Maharaja engages to disband the mutinous troops of the Lahore army, taking from them their arms; and his Highness agrees to reorganize the regular or regiments of infantry, upon the system, and according to the regulations as to pay and allowances, observed in the time of the late Maharaja Ranjit Singh. The Maharaja further engages to pay up all areas to the soldiers that are discharged under the provisions of this article.

Article 7

The regular army of Lahore State shall hence-forth by limited to 25 battalions of infantry, consisting of 800 bayonets each with 12,000 cavalry; this number at no time to be exceded without the concurrence of the British government should it be necessary at any time for any special cause, that this force should be increased, the cause shall be fully explained to the British Government, and when the special necessity shall have passed, the regular troops shall be again reduced to the standard specified in the former clause of this article.

Article 8

The Maharaja will surrender to the British Government all the guns, thirty-six in number, which have been pointed against the British troops, and which having been placed on right bank of the river Satluj, were not captured at the Battle of Sobraon.

Article 9

The control of the rivers Beas and Satluj, with the continuation of the latter river, commonly called the Ghara and Panjnad, to the confluence of the Indus from Mithankot, and the control of the Indus from Mithankot to the borders of Baluchistan, shall, in respect to tolls and ferries, rest with the British Government. The provisions of this articles shall not interfere with the passage of boats belonging to the Lahore Government on the said rivers, for the purpose of traffic or the conveyance of passengers up and down their course. Regarding the ferries between the countries respectively, at the several ghats of the said rivers, it is agreed that the British Government after defraying all the expenses of management and , establishment, shall account to the Lahore Government for one half of the net profits of the ferry collections. The provisions of this article have no reference to the ferries on that part of the river Satluj which forms the boundary of Bahawalpur and Lahore respectively.

Article 10

If the British Government should at any time, desire to pass troops through the territories of his Highness the Maharaja, for the protection of the British territories, or those of their allies, the British troops shall, on such special occasions, due notice being given, be allowed to pass through the Lahore territories. In such case, the officers of the Lahore state will afford facilities in providing supplies and boats for the passage of rivers;

and the British Government will pay the full price of all such provisions and boats, arid will make fair compensation for all private property that may be undamaged. The British Government will, moreover, observe all due consideration to the religious feelings of the inhabitants of those tracts through which the army may pass.

Article 11

The Maharaj engages never to take, or retain in his service, any British subject of any European or American State, without the consent of the British Government.

Article 12

In consideration of the services rendered by Raja Gulab Singh of Jammu to the Lahore State, towards procuring the restoration of relations of the amity between the Lahore and British Governments, the Maharaja hereby agrees to recognize the independent sovereignty of Raja Gulab Singh, in such territories and districts in the hills as may be made over to the said Raja Gulab Singh by separate agreement between himself and the British Government, with the dependencies thereof, which may have been in the Raja's possession since the time of the late Maharaja Kharak Singh; and the British Government in consideration of the good conduct of Raja Gulab Singh, also agrees to recognize his independence in -such'Territories, and to admit him to be privileges of a separate treaty with the British Government.

Article 13

In the event of any dispute of difference arising between the Lahore state and Raja Gulab Singh, the same shall be referred to the arbitration of the British Government; and by its decision the Mahraja engages to abide.

Article 14

The limits of the Lahore territories shall not be, at any time, changed without concurrence of the British Government.

Article 15

The British Government will not exercise any interference in the internal administration of the Lahore state; but in all cases or questions which may be referred to the British Government, the Governor-General will give the aid of his advice and good offices for the furtherance of the interests of the Lahore government.

Article 16

The subject of either state shall, on visiting the territories of the other, be on the footing of the subjects of the most favoured nations.

This treaty consisting of sixteen has been this day settled by Frederick Currie, Esq; and Brevet-Major Henry Montgomery Lawrence, acting under the directions of the Right Honourable Sir Henry Hardinge, GC.B., Governor-General, on the part of the British Government, and by Bhai Ram Singh, Raja Lai Singh, Sardar Tej Singh, Sardar Chattar Singh Attariwala, Sardar Ranjor Singh Manjithia, Diwan Dina Nath, and Fakir Nur-ud-din, on the part of Maharaja Dalip Singh; and the said treaty has been this day ratified by the seal of the Right Honourable Sir Henry Hardinge, G.C.B., Governor-General, and by that of His Highness Maharaja Dalip Singh.

Done at Lahore this 9th day of March in the year of our Lord 1846 corresponding with the 10 the day of Rabi-ul-awal 1262Hijri and ratified the same day.

Note:- The treaty of Lahore March 9th, 1846, is based on helpless power of Maharaja Ranjit Singh of Punjab and independent charge at that time was invested in the hands of lord Dalhousie. Whereas, the "Gulab-nama", a history of Jammu and Kashmir state was only the mission of Chritian missionery to befool the illiterate people of ladakh and Jammu region like Gulab Singh and others because the Indian had not authentic view in art of writing the subject "History"as an enquiry of the past events and study of Dalit literature = Kalhana's **Rajatarangini** (Vol. 1. p. 23).

Appendix - II

Treaty of Amritsar, 16th March, 1846

A Treaty between the British Government and Maharaja Gulab Singh was concluded at Amtirsar on 16th March, 1846. The treaty signed on the part of the British Government by Frederick Currie Esquire and Brevet major Henry Montgomery Lawrence acting under the orders of the Right Hon'ble Sir Henry Hardinge, G.C.B. one of Her Britannic Majesty's Most Honourable Privy Council, Governer-General, appointed by the Honourable Company to direct and control all their affairs in the East India and by Maharaja Gulab Singh in person. The following are the articles included in the Treart%-

1. **Article 1:** The British Government transfers and makes over, forever, in independent possession to Mahajara Gulab Singh and the heirs male of his body, all the hilly or mountainous country, with its dependencies'situated to the Eastward of the river Indus and Westward of the river Ravi, including Chamba and excluding Lahore, being part of the territory ceded to the British Government by the Lahore State according to the provisions of Articles 4 of the Treaty of Lahore dated 9th March, 1846 A.D.
2. **Articles 2:** The Eastern boundary of the tract transferred by the foregoing articles to Maharaja Gulab Singh shall be laid down by Commissioners appointed by the British Government and Maharaja Gulab Singh respectively for that purpose and shall be defined in a separate engagement after survey.
3. **Articles 3:** In consideration of the transfer made to him and his heirs by the provision of the foregoing Articles, Maharaja Gulab Singh will pay to the British Government the sum of 75 lakhs of rupees (Nanak Shahi), fifty lakhs to be paid on ratification of this Treaty and twenty-five lakhs on or before the 1st October of the current year 1846 A.D.

Appendix - III

The Delhi Agreement, 1952

The main features of this agreement are—

1. In view of the uniform and consistent stand taken up by the Jammu and Kashmir Constituent Assembly that sovereignty in all matters other than those specified in the Instrument of Accession continues to reside in the state, the Government Of India agreed that while the residuary powers of legislature vested in the centre in respect of all states other than Jammu and Kashmir, in the case of the latter they vested in the state itself;
2. It was agreed between the two Governments that in accordance with Article 5 of the Indian Constitution, persons who have their domicile in Jammu and Kashmir shall be regarded as citizens of India, but the state legislature was given power to make laws for conferring special rights and privileges on the 'state subject' in viewofthe 'State Subject' Notifications of 1927 and 1932. The State Legislature was also empowered to make laws for the 'State Subjects' who had gone to Pakistan on account of the communal disturbances of 1947, in the event of their return to Kaslunir.
3. As the President of India Commands the same respect in the state as he does in the other units of India, Article 52 to 62 of the constitution relating to him should be applicable to the state. It was further agreed that the power to grant reprieves, pardons and remission of sentences etc., would also vest in the President of India;
4. The Union Government agreed that the state should have its own flag in addition to the union flag, but it was agreed by the State Government that the state flag would not be a rival of the union flag; it was also recognised that the union flag should have the same status and position in Jammu and Kashmir as in the rest of

lndia, but for historical reasons connected with the freedom struggle in the state, the need for continuance of the state flag was recognised;

5. There was complete agreement with regard to the position of the Sadar-i-Riyasat; though the Sadar-i-Riyasat was to be elected by the State Legislature, he had to be recognised by the President of lndia before his installation as such; in other Indian States the Head of the State was appointed by the President and was as such his nominee but the person to be appointed as the Head, had to be a person acceptable to the Government of that State; no person who is not acceptable to the state Government can be thrust on the state as the Head. The difference in the case of Kashmir lies only in the fact that Sardar-i-Riyasat will in the first place be elected by the state Legislature itself instead of being a nominee of the Government and the President of India. With regard to the powers and functions of the Sadar-i-Riyasat, the following argument was mutually agreed upon-
   (a) The head of the state shall be a person recognised by the president of the union on the recommendation of the legislature of the state;
   (b) He shall hold office during the pleasure of the president.
   (c) He may, by writing under his hand addressed to the president, resign his office;
   (d) Subject to the foregoing provisions, the head of the state shall hold office for a team of five years from the date he enters upon his office;
   (e) Provided that he shal I, not with standing the expiration of his term, continue to hold the office until his successor enters upon his office;
6. With regard to the" fundamental rights, some basic principles agreed between the parties were enunciated, it was accepted that the people of the state were to have fundamental rights.

   But in view of the peculiar position in which the state was placed, the whole chapter relating to Fundamental Rights' of the Indian Constitution could not be made applicable to the state, the question which remainded to be determined-was whether the chapter of the fundamental rights should form a part of the state constitution or of the Constitution of lndia has applicable to the state;

7. With regard to the jurisdiction of the Supreme Court of India, it was accepted that for the time being, owing to the existence of the Board of Judicial Advisers in. the state, which was the highest judicial authority in the State, the Supreme Court should have only appellate jurisdiction.
8. Their was a great deal of discussion with regard to the "Emergency powers". The government of India insisted on the application of article 352, empowering the President to proclaim a general emergency in the state; the State Government argued that in the exercise of its powers over defence (Item \ on the Union List), in the event of the war or external aggression, the Government of India would have full authority to take steps and proclaimed emergency but the state delegation was, however, averse to the President exercising the power to proclaim a general emergency on account of internal disturbance.

Note:- Delhi agreement between Sheikh Abdullah and Chacha Nehru was based on 'One concept' with due respect of the coming generation, and the Supreme Power at that time was Dr. B.R. Ambedkar and how to unite the big state of India into two parts, India itself and Pakistan, it was a life-long struggle of the Dogra Ruler of Raj-Rishi (*Novel Viyogi*, Article; *Glourious History of Indus Valley civilization;* p. 1).

Appendix - IV

Memorandum of the Cabinet Mission dated 12th May, 1946 in Regard to State's Treaties and Paramountcy Paragraph 5 states:-

> When a new fully self- governing or independent Government or Governments come into being in the British India, His Majesty's Government's influence with these governments will not be such as to enable them to carry out the obligations of paramountcy. Moreover, they cannot contemplate that British troops would be retained in India for this purpose. Thus,as a logical sequence and in view of the desires expressed to them on behalf of the Indian States, His Majesty's Government will cease to exercise the power of paramountcy. This means than the rights of the states which flow from their relationship to the crown will no longer exist and all the rights surrendered by the states to the Paramount power will return to the states.Political arrangements between the states. On the one side and the British Crown and British India on the other will thus be brought to an end. The void will have to be filled either by state entering into a federal relationship with the successor Government or Governments in British India, or failing this, entering into particular political arrangements with it or them, with the efficiency of the research methods and ideology.

Note:- It was the mission of the Dalit ruler of South India that was Dr. B.R. Ambedkar and Jyoti bai Phule to provide equal status to the deprive section of the society and OBC.

Appendix - V

After his release from the imprisonment, Sheikh Mohammad Abdullah addressed a public meeting in Srinagar where he repeated the demands of the Kashmiris for 'Freedom Before Accession' in which he added emphatically.

"How can Mulsim League or Mr. Jinnah tell us that we should acceded to Pakistan? They have always opposed us in every struggle. Even in our present struggle (Quit Kashmir), he (Mr. Jinnah) carried on propaganda against us and went on saying that there was no struggle of any kind in the state. He even termed us Goondas."

As quoted by KaulandDhar, *Kashmir Speaks,* p.54 in Justice A.S. Anand, *The Constitution of Jammu and Kashmir: Its Development and Comments,* p.63 and it is found as class struggle theory of Dalits and anti-Dalits.

Note:-There is no variation in gen product of the Dalit historian, only species were converted from male to female like Bari Phalwan to Deepit Raj.

Appendix -VI

Letter dated 26th October, 1947, from Maharaja Hari Singh to Lord Mountbatten, Requesting the Accession of the State to India.

My dear Lord Mountbatten,

I have to inform your Excellency that a grave emergency has arisen in my State and request immediate assistance of your government.

As Your Excellency is aware, the State of Jammu and Kashmir has not acceded to either the Dominion of India or Pakistan. Geographically, my state is contiguous to both the Dominions. It has vital economical and cultural links with both of them. Besides my state has a common boundary with the Soviet Republic and China. In their external relations the Dominions oflndia and Pakistan cannot ignore this fact.

I wanted to take time to decide to which Dominion I should accede, whether it is not in the best interest of both the Dominions and my state to stand independent, of course,with friendly and cordial relations with both.

I accordingly approached the Dominions of India and Pakistan to enter into a stand still agreement with my state. The Pakistan Government accepted this arrangement. The Dominion of India desires further discussion with representatives of my Government. I could not arrange this in view of the developments indicated below. In fact, the Pakistan Government under the standstill agreement is operating the Post and Telegraph system inside the state.

Though we have got a standstill agreement with the Pakistan Government, that Government permitted steady and increasing strangulation of supplies like food, salt and petrol to my state.

Afridis, soldiers in plain clothes and desperadoes, with modern weapons, have been allowed to infilter into the state at first in Poonch area called "*metha family*" as a prostitute centre of the Hari Singh, that women has three sons= Rakeshas, then from Sialkot and finally in mass in the area adjoining Hazara District on the Ramkote side. The result has been that the limited number of troops at the disposal of the state has to be dispersed and thus, has to face the enemy at several points simultaneously so that it has become difficult to stop the wanton destruction of life and property and looting. The Mahoora Power House which supplies the electric current to the whole of Srinagar has been burnt. The number of women who have been kidnapped and raped makes my heart bleed. The wild forcesthus let loose on the state are marching on with the aim of capturing Srinagar, the Summer Capital of my Government, as a first step to over-running the whole-state.

The mass infiltration of tribesmen drawn from the distant areas of the North-West Frontier Province, coming regularly in motor trucks, using Mansehra-Muzaffarabad road and fully armed with up-to-date weapons cannot possibly be done without the knowledge of the Provincial Government of the North-West Frontier Province and the Government of Pakistan. Inspite of repeated appeals made by my Government, no attempt has been made to check these raiders or stop them from coining into my state. In fact, both the Pakistan Radio and press have reported these occurrences. The Pakistan Radio even put out a story that a Provisional Government has been set up in Kashmir. The people of my state both Muslims and non-Muslims generally have taken no part at all.

With the conditions obtaining at present in my state and the great emergency of the situation as it exists, I have no option but to ask for help from the Indian Dominion. Naturally they cannot send the help asked for by me without my state acceding to the Dominion of India. I have accordingly decided to do so, and 1 attach the Instrument of Accession for acceptance by your Government. The other alternative is to leave my state and my people to free-booters. On tins basis, no civilized Government can exist or be maintained. This alternative I will never allow to happen so long as I am the Ruler of the State and I have life to defend my country.

I may also inform your Excellency's Government that it is my intention at once to set up an Interim Government and ask Sheikh Abdullah to carry the responsiblites in this emergency with my Prime-Minister.

If my state has to be saved, immediate assistance must be available at Srinagar, Mr. V.P. Menon is fully aware of the situation and he will explain to you, if further explanation is needed.

In haste and with kindest regards.

Yours Sincerely
Hari Singh

Note:- Salinder Singh Jamwal, Ex-HOD History, become the slave of the author as Snake Value of the modern studies. Rajput history stands nowhere without knowing the Dalit concept as fictions literature of the S.D.S. Charak and M.L. Kapur = Collection base knowledge = strong Brahminmat of North India (J&K State).

Appendix-VII

List of Govenors of Jammu and Kashmir State

S. No.	Name	Took Offices as Governors	Left Offices
1.	Maj Pritam Singh Jamwal	1940	1948
2.	Yuvraj Dr. Karan Singh	30,b March, 1965	15th May, 1967
3.	Bhagwan Sahay	15th May, 1967	3rd July, 1973
4.	LakshmiKantJha	3ri July, 1973	22nd Feb, 1981
5.	Braj Kumar Nehru	22ndFeb, 1981	26th April, 1984
6.	JagMohan	26th April, 1984	July, 1989
7.	K.V. Krishna Rao	July 1989	19th January, 1990
8.	Jag Mohan	19th January, 1990	26th May, 1990
9.	Girish Chander Saxena	26th May, 1990	12th March, 1993
10.	K.V. Krishna Rao	12th March, 1993	2nd May, 1998
11.	Girish Chander Saxena	2nd May, 1998	4th June, 2003
12.	S.K. Sinha	4th June, 2003	24* June, 2008
13.	NarinderNath Volira	25th June, 2005	Till Date

Appendix - VIII

List of Chief Ministers of Jammu and Kashmir

S.No.	Name	Term	Party
1	Gulam Mohammad Sadiq Congress	30th March 1965-12th Dec 1971	Indian National
2	Syed Mir Qasim Congress	12th Dec 1971 -25th Feb 1975	Indian National
3	SheikhMohammad Abdullah	25th Feb 1975-26th March 1977	National Conference
4	President's Rule	26th March 1977-9th July 1977	-
5	Sheikh M. Abdullah	9th July 1977-8th Sept 1982	National Conference
6	Dr. Farooq Abdullah	8th Sept 1982- 2nd July 1984	National Conference
7	Gulam Mohammad Shah	2nd July 1984-8th March 1986	Awami National Conference
·	President's Rule	6th March 1986-7th Nov. 1986	-
8	Dr. Farooq Abdullah	7th Nov. 1986-19th Jan 1990	National Conference
·	President's Rule	19th Jan 1990-9th Oct 1996	-
9	Dr. Frooq Abdullah	9th Oct 1996-18th Oct 2002	National Conference
•	President's Rule	18th Oct2002-2nd Nov. 2002	-
10	Mufti Mohammad Sayeed	2ndNov.2002-2nd Nov. 2005	People's Democratic Party (PDP)
11	Gulam NabiAzad	2ndNov.^005-ll* July 2008	Congress I
•	President's Rule	11 * July 2008-5*January 2009	—
12	Omar Abdullah	5*January 2009-8*January 2015	National Conference
13	Mufti Mohd. Sayeed	1st March 2015- 8* Jan 2016	P.D.P.
14	Ms. Mehbooba Mufti	4th April 2016 to Till Today	P.D.P.

Appendix- IX

Name of 87 Constituencies of State Legislative Assembly of J&K

1.	Akhnoor	25.	Ganderbal
2.	Amira Kadal	26.	Gandhi Nagar
3.	Anantnag	27.	GoolArnas
4.	Bandipora	28.	GulabGarh
5.	Bani	29.	Gulmarg
6.	Banihal	30.	Gurez
7.	Baramulla	31.	Habba Kadal
8.	Basholi	32.	Handwara
9.	Batmaloo	33.	Hazratbal
10.	Beerwah	34.	Hiranagar
11.	Bhaderwah	35.	Homshalibugh
12.	Bijbehara	36.	Inderwal
13.	Billawar	37.	Jammu East
14.	Bishnah	38.	Jammu West
15.	Budgam	39.	Kala kote
16.	Chadoora	40.	Kangan
17,	Chenani	41.	Kargil
18.	Chammb	42.	Karnah
19.	Charar-i-Sharif	43.	Kathua
20.	Darhal	44.	Khan Sahib
21.	Devsar	45.	Khanyar
22.	Doda	46.	Kishtwar
23.	Doora	47.	Kokernag
24.	Eidgali	48.	Kulgam
49.	Kupwara	69.	Ram ban
50.	Langate	70.	R.S.Pura
51.	Leh	71.	Reasi
52.	Lolab	72.	Samba
53.	Marh	73.	Sangrama

(Contd...)

54.	Mendhar	74.	Shangus
55.	Nagrota	75.	Shopian
56.	Nooorabad	76.	Sonawar
57.	Nowshera	77.	Sonawari
58.	Nubra	78.	Sopore
59.	Pehalgam	79.	Suchet Garh
60.	Pampore	80.	Surankote
61.	Pattan	81.	Tral
62.	Poonch Haveli	82.	Udhampur
63.	Pulwama	83.	Uri
64.	Rafiabad	84.	Vijaypur
65.	Raipur Domana	85.	Wachi
66.	Rajouri	86.	Zadibal
67.	Rajpora	87.	Zanskar
68.	Ram Nagar		

Appendix-X

List of Chief Justice of J&K High Court

S.No.	Chief Justice	Term
1.	Kanwar Sain	27 th April 1928-16 th Feb 1931
2.	BirjorSain	16 th Febl931-24 th Novl936
3.	Abdul Qayoom	24th Nov.l936-20 th July 1940
4.	Rachpal Singh	13 th August 1940-6th March 1942
5.	Ganga Nath	24th June 1942-29 th March 1946
6.	S.K. Ghose	29 th March 1946-29th March 1948
7.	JankiNathWazir	30th March 1948-2ndDec 1967
8.	Sayed MurtazaFaziAli	3rd Dec 1967-l st April 1975
9.	Raja Jaswant Singh	2nd April 1975-23rd January 1976
10.	MRA Ansari	23rd Jan 1976-8 th Nov. 1977
11.	Mian Jalal-ul-Din	15th Feb.1978-22nd Feb 1980
12.	Mufti Bah-ud-Din	7th March 1983-23rd August 1983
13.	V. Angarial Kbahid	24th August 1983-24th June 1984
14.	Adarsh Sein Anand	11th May 1985-23rd Oct 1989
15.	S.S.Kang	24th Oct 1989-14 th Mayl993
16.	S.C. Mathur	10 th Oct 1993- 17 th Marchl.994
17.	S. Sagir Ahmed	18th March 1994-22nd Sept. 1994
18.	M.Ramakrishna	10 th Oct 1994-15 th June 1997
19.	Bhawani Singh	16 th June 1997-21st Feb 2000
20.	B.P.Saraf	21st Feb 2000-22nd August 2001
21.	H.K. Sema	12th Sept.2001 -8th April 2002
22.	B.C.Patel	16th May 2002-4th March2003
23.	S.N. Jha	4th Feb2004-11 th Oct2005
24.	B.A. Khan	25 th Jan 2007-31 th March 2007
25.	Aftab Alam	7 th June 2007-10 th Nov 2007
26.	K.S. Radhakrishnan	7th January 2.008-28 th August 2008
27.	Manmohan Sarin	4 th Sept. 2008-19 th Oct 2008
28.	Barin Ghosh	3rd Jan 2009-13 th April 2010
29.	Dr. Justice Aftab Hussain Saikia	13 th April 2010-6 th April 2011
30	FM Ibrahim Khalifulla	24 th Feb2011-2ndApril2012
31	Mahesh Mittal Kumar	8 th June2012-4 th Jan2015
32	N.Paul Vasantha Kumar	2nd Feb 2015-Till date

Appendix-XI

Gajendragadkar Commission

Note: The State Government of Jammu & Kashmir had appointed P.B. Gajendragadkar as the head of J&K Commission of Inquiry in 1967. This Commission was to make an assessment of the developmental programmes undertaken in various regions of the State, to examine the recruitment policies of the government, to examme the policies of the State Government regarding admissions to the institutions of higher education and the scholarships and loans and to consider generally the causes that lead to regional irritations and tensions and also to recommend remedial measures. The following were the important principal findings of the Gajendragadkar Commission-

Development Programmes

While the resources of the Jammu and Kashmir region were equal, the share of the later in developmental expenditure within the plans was 22% higher than that of the former. Ladakh, which had scanty resources and required a great deal of additional support from the State and the Union Government received a much small share than either the Jammu region or the Kashmir region. So far as non-plan expenditure during the second and third plan periods was concerned, Ladakh's share had only been one fourth of the Jammu and Kashmir region.

However, the Commission pointed out the major regional disparities occurred in the field of agriculture, irrigation, power, transport and communication, education and health and family planning. Although, the gross area under cultivation in Jammu region was much larger than that of Kashmir region, yet in investment in agriculture the share of former had been substantially less as compared to the later. In Ladakh on the other hand, it remained almost static.

So for as the availability of irrigation facilities were concerned, the Kashmir region was much better served than Jammu or Ladakh. Moreover, by the end of third plan period, the availability of power in Kashmir region was also considerably more than in Jammu region. In other words, the number of town and villages electrified in Kashmir region were almost double than that of Jammu. But in Ladakh, it was almost negligible. As for as transport and communication was concerned, Ladakh region suffered most. A number of roads, though constructed in the area yet, the public transport facilities still remained unsatisfactory there.

In case of educational development, the Kashmir region had done better than the other two regions. The student teacher ratio for high and higher secondary schools though smaller in Kashmir region as compared to Jammu region, yet the enrolment in colleges in Kashmir region was almost twice than that of Jammu region. Moreover, the professional institutions were mostly located in Kashmir region. The Agricultural College at R.S. Pura (in Jammu region) had since been ordered to be closed. In Ladakh, the health and family planning facilities available then appeared to be extremely poor as compared with other two regions. In short, the development expenditure in the Plan period incurred in Kashmir region had been more (22%) than that of incurred in Jammu region. While taking in account the developmental expenditure incurred outside the plan, some kind of similar arithmetical parity between the regions could also be established.

Recruitment Policies

Though, the population of Kashmir region was 53.3% of the total population of the state, its share in the services on April 1, 1967 was 60.9%. The population of Jammu region on the other hand was 42.2% of the total population of the state but its share in the services on April 1,1967 was only 36.1%. The rate of recruitment of Ladakhis had shown a decline from2.5% in 1961-62 to 1.4% in 1964-66.

The community wise position was that the Muslims had shown an improvement through their total share of services but still less than, what it should be on the basis of population. Hindus share in the services had shown decline, but it was much higher, what was due to them on the basis of population. The Buddhists had also shown a fall, but the recruitment of the Sikhs in the services had been fluctuating from year to year and its share on April 1, 1967 was considerably in excess what was due to them on the basis of population.

Educational Policies

The number of students belonging to Jammu, selected for studies in higher institutions was much smaller than that of Kashmir region. Moreover, the students belonging to Kashmir region had received a higher amount by way of study loans than that of the students of Jammu region. The Commission, therefore, recommended that there should be a statutory State Development Board, and Regional Development Board for three regions-Jammu, Kashmir and Ladakh. The Regional Board should be headed by the Chief Minister or the Planning Minister and should consist of the Legislators from the regions, economists experts and concerned officials. The regions should be adequately represented on the State Development Board which should be headed by the Chief Minister. This Board should draw up the regional plans, to assign priority to scheme and projects and to supervise the implementation of regional plans. The Board should pay due regard to the special needs of the backward areas of their respective regions. The State Development Board should be headed by the Chief Minister and be adequately represented by the regions. It should scrutinize the regional plans, prepare a residuary plan of schemes and projects which transcend regional boundaries or happened to be of all State level and al locate plan funds equitably.

The State Development Board and each of the Regional Development Board should prepare at the end of each year a report of their respective activities giving details of the progress of the plan programmes and plan expenditure. At the end of each plan, similar detailed reports should be prepares by the Boards indicating the physical and financial targets and the physical and financial achievements. All these reports should be laid before the Legislature as .soon as may be after they are prepared.

Recruitment rules for all the state services for which they do not exist at present should be framed and promulgated as early as possible. Recruitment rules for other services also should be speedily framed. The following multiple criteria should be treated as backward:

(a) The occupation or occupations pursed by that class of citizens.

(b) Their place of habitation.

(c) The average of student population per thousand in that class.

Reservation of services to be made for backward class in proportion to their population but it should not exceed 50%. Similarly, reservation for backward classes and scheduled castes be made in educational and professional institutions. There should also be provision for scholarship and study loans for them.

A convention should be established that if the Chief Minister belonged to one region, there should be Deputy Chief Minister from the other, the number of Cabinet Ministers belonging to the two regions should be equal and a full-fledged Cabinet Minister belonging to Ladakh. The functions of each Head of Department should be divided on regional basis, having a Head and Additional Head one of them functioning in one region and the other in the other region. The department will be under the overall control of main head who will also be responsible for the coordination of work between him and Additional Head. When the High Court of J&K would function at Srinagar, there should be at least one High Court Judge stationed at Jammu. Similarly, one High Court Judge should be stationed at Srinagar in winter.

Some of the cadres should be district based, certain others region based and the balance state based. In district based cadres transfers should be only within districts whereas in the region-based transfers should be permissible only within the region. But members of State based cadres alone should be transferable anywhere within the state. The inferior and non-gazetted transferable posts (other than supervisory) should be district based non-supervisory non-gazetted both clerical and non-clerical should be in regional cadres and class III and class IV gazetted posts should be in the regional cadre. But the residents of the entire state should be eligible for appointment to the posts including in any of these cadres.

The members of the K.A.S, K.C.S (Judicial), K.P.S, and much other state services as the state government may consider necessary, shall be liable to serve for a minimum specific period (say, 5 years in each of the three regions of Jammu, Kashmir and Ladakh).

A Regional Recruitment Board, to make recruitment to the regional cadres, to set up for each of the Jammu, Kashmir and Ladakh. A District Cadres should be set up for each district in the state including Ladakh. These Boards would fill up those posts which would be outside the purview of P.S.C.

There should be a separate full-fledged University in both Jammu and Kashmir regions. One of them, preferably in Jammu, should immediately start a faculty of law. Subsequently, law classes will also have to be started in the other University. As all the professional colleges were located in Kashmir it would be proper to open a new Medical College in Jammu.

The question of starting an Engineering College in Jammu region might be considered when the need for the large number of engineer graduates was felt. A Degree College should be established immediately at Leh. Subsequently, a college should also be established at Kargil, then Zanskar and Nobra.

The Government should review the entire policy of food grain prices, both for procurement and for issue, and should introduce uniform grain policy throughout the Jammu and Kashmir regions. The quantum of ration issued at Srinagar and Jammu should also be uniform. In the Ladakh district too no distinction should be made between locals and non-locals government servants in the matter of ration allocation. The non-locals should be permitted to take the whole or part of the rice in the form of wheat flour, if they so desired.

The status of Leh should be accorded due recognition as the headquarters of a vast region by the construction of suitable buildings and roads and provision of sanitary arrangements and other such measures. The State Government should also consider the request of the people of Ladakh for giving Ladakh its due place in the formal name of the state. The single-line administration should also be revived in its entirety in Ladakh. The Deputy Commissioner should function as ahead of all departments in Ladakh and Ladakh Affairs Secretary should be Secretary for all subjects. He should work under the Minister of Ladakh Affairs and JKLF ke Study.

Note: History of Ladakh is based on honoest living apporach as Dalit literature of the Buddhist philisophy. (Dr. Raj Kumar; **"A Complete History of Jammu and Kashmir State";** pp. 215-248).

Appendix - XII

Sikri Commission: Commission of Inquiry = Dalit Literature of the Northern States of India after 1947 to 2017

The State Government of Jammu and Kashmir appointed a Commission of Inquiry about the question of regional imbalances as well as imbalances among the various district administrative units within the region on 2nd June, 1979. It was headed by Justice S.M.Sikri retired Chief Justice of Supreme Court and including Malcolm Adiseshia and A.R.Kidwai. Later on, Kidwai VC of Haryana University as the followers of Ambedkar thought and translated a book on Malka Pukraj called Preety Bhagat at Present was replaced by M.Zaheer who also acted as the secretary of the Commission.

The following were the important findings after investigating the grievances of three regions:—

Developmental Programmes

Many areas of state were, as cut off, isolated and poor as they were at the dawn of independence, Commission found it necessary to improve the living standards of all those areas which were backward, especially having the sections like Scheduled Castes, Gujjars, Backwards etc. Keeping all this in view, Ladakh region needed a visible acceleration of the tempo of its development. In the field of employment status, Commission found that Ladakh had the highest percentage of workers to the population of the region in 1971 with a lowest dependency ratio in terms of non-workers as compared to Jammu and Kashmir regions where every worker had to support 24 non-workers Kashmir region had the largest work force among the three regions. The State Director of Evaluation and Statistics reported that the number of educated unemployed had increased from 15,321 in 1970 to

44,374 in March 31,1978 and that the problem was more acute in Kashmir than in Jammu.

In response to the number and area of holdings the Commission found, on the basis of agricultural census of 1971, that Kashmir had double the number of marginal holdings as compared to Jammu, while Ladakh had more than half of its total holdings in this group. Jammu had double in number of medium holdings and triple the number of large holdings compared to Kashmir. While Ladakh had very little in this respect. In regards to small holdings Jammu had less than one third more such holdings compared to Kashmir and Ladakh.

The area under orchards cultivation between the year 1966-67 and 1977-78 showed that Kashmir region had the natural (climate and soil) advantage over the other two regions in the respect. The area under cultivation had increased in Jammu and marginally in Ladakh having a decline in Kashmir. The total and annual average expenditure on soil conservation showed an imbalance between Jammu and Kashmir region, with Jammu region spending double than that of Kashmir region.

From 1974 to 1978, the live stock population of the state in regards to region showed that Kashmir with a large human population had a smaller total live stock population and about half per hundred inhabitants compared to Jammu. This was on account of the larger plan expenditure, both total and annual average in Kashmir over Jammu and the near equal number of annual hospitals in the two regions. The decline in the total and per hundred inhabitants of the live stock population in Ladakh region was an imbalance which needed investigation.

In the field of forest development expenditure, the imbalance was in the favour of Jammu region, Jammu region had 33% more forest area than Kashmir, but on which about double development expenditure and 52% more of per hundred hectare expenditure had been incurred compared to the expenditure in Kashmir. Ladakh's figures were not comparable because of little forests there.

In the field of irrigation, the Commission found that between regions (a) the net sown area increased during the fourth and the fifth plan in Jammu was near stagnant in Ladakh and increased marginally in Kashmir; and (b) the net irrigated area both in absolute terms and as percentage of net area sown rose by a third to a half in Jammu, remained stagnant in Ladakh and fall in Kashmir. Imbalances were also reflected in the expenditures on irrigation, total and annual average as between the regions with 68% increase in Jammu over Kashmir.

So far as Industries were concerned, Jammu had 37% more units than Kashmir, with 37% more fixed capital investment with the value of output of its units over four times greater than that of Kashmir. There was no such unit in Ladakh.

Considering education, an important development indicator, the Commission found (a) a higher rate of increase of primary and secondary schools in Jammu over Kashmir and Ladakh, (b) a hi glier percentage of the relevant age group at all levels of Middle and Secondary schooling in Ladakh, (d) a higher teacher-pupil ratio in Jammu compared to Kashmir and Ladakh, and lack of any college facilities in Ladakh region.

However, Commission found a serious imbalance in drinking water facilities faced by Ladakh where only 1/30 of the villages had drinking water facilities and Jammu region's annual rate of provision was about half of the Kashmir region. Again, Ladakh faced an imbalance in both, surfaced and unsurfaced roads even allowing the fact that a large part of the .area was uninhabited Jammu also faced ar. imbalance in this respect as compared to Kashmir.

The allocation of financial resources as based on Gadgil formula showed that in 1978-79 Jammu had been given 7% more than its share, Kashmir 16% less and Ladakh 3 7% more than the allocation based on population parity.

Recruitment Policies

Second term of reference to the Commission was to examine the recruitment policies of the Government and to recommend constitutional measures to ensure an equitable share of the different regions in the government employment. In order to simplify the analysis, the government servents were compressed into the following three categories:—

1. Gazetted
2. Non-gazetted
3. Class IV

So far as the functioning of the Public Service Commission was concerned, the allegations were made that it could not function independently and in accordance with the norms in dealing with services. In order to investigate the matter, the Commission received the reports, of the Public Service Commission from 1967-68 to 1976-77 and found the following irregularities:—

1. Non availability of Annual Charter Recruitment Rules.

2. Non-acceptance or partial acceptance of recommendation of the Commission.
3. Appointments made, without consulting the Commission as well as to make appointments in contravention of rules.
4. Adhoc appointments made by the government without consulting the Commission
5. Appointment made but cases not referred to the Commission during the year 1973-74to 1976-77.

Again, dealing with the complaints made in regards to the working of the District, Regional and State Recruitment Boards, Commission wanted an improvement in the working of those boards in order to foster the confidence of the general public in these recruiting bodies.

Professional Institutions and Their Admission

Professional institutions in the state fall under three disciplines viz. (i) Engineer, (ii) Agriculture, (iii) Medical, (iv) Acadmicans are found in large number in SC/ST of the J&K State.

There are only six professional institutions in the state, four in Srinagar (Polytechnics, Regional Engineering College, Agricultural College, Medical College) and two in Jammu (Polytechnic and Medical). There is no professional college in Ladakh region. The data provided to the Commission showed that from 1974 to 1978 in Polytechnic College at Jammu, there were 465 students from Jammu region, 29 from Kashmir region and 5 from Ladakh region. In Kashmir Polytechnic, there were 18 students from Jammu region, 395 from Kashmir and 5 from Ladakh region.

During the same period, Agriculture College, Sopore got admitted 91 students from Jammu region 191 from Kashmir and 8 from Ladakh region. In the Regional Engineering College Srinagar from 1968-79,385 students got admission from Jammu region, 864 from Kashmir and 20 from Ladakh region. Admission to medical College Srinagar and Jammu from 1974-1978 showed that there were 25 and 27 students from Jammu region, 387 and 14 from Kashmir region and 18 and 6 from Ladakh region respectively.

The imbalances of two regions of the state in different catagories of state services are reflected in the recommendation of the Commission.

In order to study the correct development imbalances, the Commission recommended the government to compile figures of per-capita income at current prices by regions and district administrative units and undertake studies which will indicate per capita expenditure by fractile distribution of the population in the state, region and district administrative units, using as appropriate the survey that National Sample Survey and Reserve Bank of India undertake.

Regions and districts should compile periodically the data in respect of the number of under employed and unemployed both literate and illiterate so that the employment generation programme may be related to regional and district development activities. The decline in live stock population as compared to inhabitants in Poonch, Rajouri, Leh and Kargil needs investigation. Law expenditure in the field of irrigation in Kashmir region, backward areas of Poonch, Rajouri, Dpda and Mahore of Udhampur reflected imbalances. Special attention was also demanded in irrigation Baramulla. Further investments should be made in electrification of the villages of Rajouri and Doda. Availability of power in the regions of Ladakh needs augmentation. Attention should be made to set up small industrial units in Ladakh, Qoda, Rajouri and Poonch which suffer from serious imbalances in thty respect.

Drinking water facilities, setting up of housing colonies, development of roads in Ladakh region, Doda, Rajouri, Poonch, Kupwara needed to be improved. Programmes and projects for correction of imbalance as between districts and in backward areas already identified should be incorporated in the State plan documents. The additional allocation made for backward areas must be spent exclusively oh tiiese areas and not diverted either to the common pool of region or to other areas. The imbalances favouring Leh against Kargil needs correction.

In the case of Ladakh and other areas with short working season, the allotment of funds should be made on a two year basis. The Commission recommended reservation in services for scheduled caste on the basis of population for the State as a whole and not at the district level. The trend of improvement in representation in services of the residents of Jammu region may be kept up consistent with the maintenance of efficiency in administration. Local candidates should be given preference in the recruitment of all posts in class IV at the district and divisional level.

In order to provide better representation from rural area, the promising students from all such areas should be picked up and groomed for competition with other for entry into government services. Government may not encroach on the sphere of activity entrusted to the PSC unless absolutely unavoidable in which case it should give' its reasons in writing.

Again, there should be no interference in the functioning of the district and divisional recruitment boards. Statistics of admission should be compiled by district of residence in order to remove imbalances if any.

The via-voce test for admission into professional institutions should be done away with, and the admissions to Medical College should be conducted for both colleges jointly. Admission to Polytechnics, Agriculture Colleges and Regional Engineering College should be made solely on the basis of marks obtained at the qualifying examination which is conducted by a common Board for the entire state.

A State Development Board may be set up, composed of the Chief Minister as Chairman and some members of the State Legislature as members, and may be entrusted with supervision over the working of district development boards formulation of allocation of funds for developmental expenditure, ensuring selection of meritorious boys and girls for special educational facilities and to report annually to the legislature on the working of the District Development Boards.

Note: Dalit literature is based on historical research of Kalhana's Rajatarangini = Kashmir Issue + Secondary sources of the Dalit Assertion in Society = Women History ka literature Dr. (Prof.) Renu Angurana, as an efficient lady; but at the same time she has been caught by the dogs day study. (Imtiaz Ahmad & S.B. Upadhyay; **"Dalit Assertion in Society; Literatures and History";** pp. 1-20).

Appendix - XIII

Uncip Resolution of January 5, 1949

The United Nations Commission for India and Pakistan

Having received from the Government of India and Pakistan, in communications dated 23rd December and 25th December 1948, respectively, their acceptance of the following principles which are supplementary to the Commission's Resolution of 13th August 1948.

1. The question of the accession of the State of Jammu and Kashmir to India or Pakistan will be decided through the democratic method of a free and impartial plebiscite.
2. A plebiscite will be held when it shall be found by the Commission that the cease-fire and truce arrangements set forth in Parts I and II of the commission's resolution of 3th August 1948, have been carried out and arrangements for the plebiscite have been completed.
3. (a) The secretary-General of the United Nation will, in agreement with the Commission, nominate a Plebiscite Administrator who shall be a personality of high international standing and commanding general confidence. He will be formally appointed to the office by the government of Jammu and Kashmir.

   (b) The Plebiscite Administrator shall derive from the State of Jammu and Kashmir the powers he considers necessary for organizing and conducting the plebiscite and for ensuring the freedom and impartiality of the plebiscite.

   (c) The Plebiscite Administrator shall have authority to appoint such staff of assistants and observers as he may require.
4. (a) After implementation of part I and III of the commission's resolution of 13th August, 1948 and when the Commission is satisfied that peaceful conditions have been restored in the state,

the Commission and the Plebiscite Administrator will determine, in consultation with the Government of India, the final disposal of Indian and the state armed forces, such disposal to be with due regard to the security of the state and freedom of the plebiscite, (b) As regards the territory referred to in 2A of part II of the resolution of 13th August, final disposal of the armed forces in that territory will be determined by the Commission and the Plebiscite Administrator in consultation with the local authorities.

5. All civil and military authorities within the state and the principal political elements of the state will be required to co-operate with the Plebiscite Administrator in the preparation for and the holding of the Plebiscite.

6. (a) All citizens of the state who have left it on account of the disturbances will be invited and be free to return and to exercise all their rights as such citizens. For the purpose of facilitating repatriation, there shall be appointed two Commissions, one composed of nominees of India and the other of nominees of Pakistan, The Commission shall operate under the direction of the Plebiscite Administrator. The Government oflndia and Pakistan and all authorities within the state of Jammu and Kashmir will collaborate with the Plebiscite Administrator in putting this provision into effect.

   (b) All persons (other than citizen of the state) who on or since 15th August, 1947 have entered it for other than lawful purpose, shall be required to leave the state.

7. All authorities within the state of Jammu and Kashmir will undertake to ensure, in collaboration with the Plebiscite Administrator, that,

   (a) There is no threat, coercion or intimidation, bribery or other undue influence on the voters in the plebiscite;

   (b) No restrictions are placed on legitimate political activity throughout the state. All subjects of the state, regardless of creed, caste or part, shall be safe and free in expressing their views and in voting on the question of accession of the state to India or Pakistan. There shall be freedom of the press, speech and assembly and freedom of travel in the state, including freedom of lawful entry and exist;

   (c) All political prisoners are released;

(d) Minorities in all parts of the state are accorded adequate protection; and

(e) There is no victimization.

8. The Plebiscite Administrator may refer to the United Nations Commission for the India and Pakistan problems on which he may require assistance, and the commission may in its discretion call upon the Plebiscite Administrator to carry out on its behalf any of the responsibilities with which it has been entrusted.
9. At the conclusion of the Plebiscite, the Plebiscite Administrator shall report the result thereof to the Commission and to the Government of Jammu and Kashmir. The Commission shall then certify to the Security Council whether the Plebiscite has or has not been free and impartial.
10. Upon the signature of truce agreement the details of the forgoing proposals will be elaborated in the consultation envisaged in Part III of the Commission's resolution of 13th August, 1948. The Plebiscite Administrator will be fully associated in these consultations.

Commands the Government oflndia and Pakistan for the prompt action in ordering a cease-fire to take effect from one minute before midnight of January 1, 1949, pursuant to the agreement arrived at as provided for by the Commission's resolution of 13th August 1948; and Resolves to return in the immediate future to the subcontinent of discharge the responsibilities imposed upon it by the resolution of 13th August, 1948 and by the forgoing principles and Dying village Bhauana Chock ke History = Thakur + Chamar history ka literature = One Concept = Nam – History. **Note:** Frontline Magazine dated March 4, 2016 = the same story as Dalit Studies = Chamar – thought. (p. 1-2).

Appendix - XIV

Mohtarma Mehbooba Mufti Sahiba,

The Hon'ble Chief Minister,

Jammu & Kashmir State

Sub: Memorandum of demands.

Hon'ble Madam Sahiba,

Ours is a non political organization working for the upliftment of weaker sections like SCs/STs/OBCs, ensuring their share in the governance of affairs of the state and protection of their constitutional rights. The Reservation Act, 2004, SRO-144 of 2008, SRO 110 of 2000, one step up Reservation in Promotion and some other welfare measures in the state are at the credit of the state unit of the Confederation. We the office bearers of confederation belonging to all districts, tehsil and blocks have assembled today on 16-01-2017 for a peaceful march in Jammu thereby making a collective effort to cite and discern our concern over the pathetic condition of SC/ST/OBC's of the state and by medium of this memorandum, we hereby draw your kind attention to the burning issues confronted by the SC/ST/OBC's of the state and request your Hon'ble self to ensure immediate redressal for the same. Through the medium of this memorandum we wish to submit the following issues for your kind consideration:

1. **Restoration of Reservation:** There is 'Reservation' in promotion only upto Deputy Secretary and equivalent post. Reservations in recruitments and promotions are granted to ensure participation of weaker sections like SCs/STs/OBCs in the governance of affairs of the state and to help their community masses to get fair justice. Recently, in the wake of Hon'ble High Court of J&K High Court having given contradictory directions regarding reservation in promotions, the government ought to have immediately come up with following solutions to protect their own reservation act and rules.

   (a) promulgating an ordinance to incorporate the provisions of reservation in promotion to negate the judgment passed by the

Hon'ble High Court. The Reservation Act, 2004 was passed during the Chief ministership of Late Jenab Mufti Mohammed Sayeed Sahib. These communities have been gravely prejudiced by the said judgment and subsequent inaction of the government. Reincorporation of provisions in Reservation Act and rules thereunder for providing reservation in promotions by way of amendment in the said Act is the need of the hour.

2. **Clearing backlog of vacancies:** There are about five lacs employees in the state govt. Share of SCs/STs/OBCs comes to 40,000/50,000/10,000 respectively but there are only 17000 SCs, 34000 STs and 5000 **OBC** employees in the state, who are mostly class IV employees. Accordingly the backlog comes to 23000 for SCs, 18000 for STs and 5000 for OBCs. These backlog vacancies should be filled through special recruitment drive.
3. **Share in Adhoc/contractual daily wager appointments:** There are about 61000 adhoc/ contractual daily wagers and share of **SCs/** STs/ OBCs comes to 4880 for SCs, 6100 for SYs and 1220 for OBCs which may be granted to these weaker sections.
4. **Scholarship for SC/ST/OBC students:** Scholarship to **SC**/ST/ OBC students are either not paid or paid too late. There is backlog of 3 years in payment of scholarships to these students of weaker sections. There is need of paying special attention for timely payment of scholarships. Admission fee of scholarship getting students can be adjusted against scholarship to be paid to them to mitigate their sufferings.
5. **Implementation** of **27% reservation for OBC's:** as promised by **ex-CM** of the state as per the recommendations of the Mandal Commission report duly confirmed by the Hon'ble Supreme Court in Indira Sawhney**'s case** OBC**'s** are entitled to 27 percent reservation. Further, the Confederation demands enhancement of income slab for the OBC**'s** at par with that at the centre for creamy layer.
6. **Dilution of ST status:** Govt, should stop the attempts being made to include some other affluent classes under ST category. These people are already getting benefit of reservation under RBA category and should not **be** included under ST category.
7. **State budgetary allocation for special component plan:** Special Component plan for SC's and ST's should be adequately provisioned **and** the same **be** strictly utilized for generating job

avenues for these communities so that inclination of unemployed youth towards public employment is lessened. Accountability should be fixed for utilization of funds under special component plans of the **state** which are exclusively meant for income generating programs for SC/ST/OBC**'s** and for stopping diversion thereof for general purposes.

8. **Providing shelter homes:** Shelter homes to homeless SC/ST/OBC may be provided. They are not granted assistance under IAY scheme on one pretext or the other.
9. **Providing equal opportunities to SC/ST/OBC's in the matter of posting/transfers:** Instances are galore where the Government, while placing officials in the rotate, overlooks those belonging to SCs/STs/OBC's for posting/placement on posts of public importance. In Spite of officials belonging to these categories being senior, are overlooked and made to work under those belonging to other general communities, even though juniors. Such actions by the government are bound to create an impression of deliberate insult to such officials because of their belonging to these communities.
10. **Political Reservation to STs:** Political reservation to STs may be granted to ensure their representation in the Legislature.
11. **Devising mechanism for redressal of atrocities upon SC/ST/OBC's and extension of jurisdiction of National Commission for SC and ST's to the J&K State:** in order to provide speedy justice to the SC/ST/OBC people who are victimized due to any reason whatsoever, a special monitoring mechanism, with senior officers having quasi judicial powers, should **be** set up and their complaints should be redressed in a time bound manner. Moreover, this issue can also be taken care of adequately by extending the jurisdiction of National Commission for Scheduled Castes and that for the Scheduled Tribes to the State of J&K.
12. **Opening of Special Police Stations for Scheduled Castes and Scheduled Tribes in every district:** It shall also counter the menace of caste based and status based discrimination and ostracisation.
13. **Extension of SC, ST (Prevention of Atrocities) Act, 1989:** to the state of Jammu and Kashmir as the present legal mechanism of the state is not adequate to meet the violations and-offences committed against these communities.

14. **Reservation in private sector:** For SC/ST/OBc's as the government has either outsourced some of its functions or has converted government departments into corporations and companies with minority shareholding where reservation is not made applicable, as such, it is imperative that reservation is provided to SC/ST/OBC's in private sector.
15. **Opening** of result **oriented coaching centres for All India Services:** Coaching centres for the SC/ST/OBC's for preparation of All India services may be opened as these candidates cannot afford to take coaching at private coaching centres, even if competent, they are unable to make the grade in view of every well to do candidate having availed professional coaching for these services. To raise the level of these candidates, professional coaching centers are need of the hour.
16. **New Schemes for Wattal/safai karamcharis:** Institute new schemes for these communities and provide them with modern instruments and educational facilities so that these communities can be saved from manual scavenging and menial jobs. Also, they should be permanently employed in their jobs and their children should be provided special avenues in education and mainstream employment so that they saved from doing this degrading work and contribute to nation building. Special camps should be held by the government in every district for creating awareness among them and for providing them with infrastructural facilities for their upliftment.

In the light of the above stated demands, which also serve the purpose of apprising your Hon'ble self regarding the deplorable condition of SC/ST/OBC's and other reserved categories and snatching away of their rights guaranteed by the constitution itself, it is therefore strongly demanded that the above said issues be sorted out at the earliest. It is a primary issue for good governance that the most deprived of the sections must be given primacy and pushed upwards so that they contribute equally to the development of the state. We expect that your Hon'ble self, being the first woman Chief Minister of the state, shall definitely understand the plight of SC/ST/OBC's and other reserved categories of the state and an affirmative action in the light of afore stated demands shall be taken by the government headed by your Hon'ble self at the earliest.

We the office bearers of state, district, tehsil and blocks thus present this memorandum for your kind consideration at an earliest. From the study, we learn that Dalits from the Jammu and Kashmir State as well as of Southern Indian, they are efficient works of the lord, Dera Barnai (R.L. Kalsotra; President, SC/ST/OBC, J&K State) and are working with the positive manners with ideology of Dr. B.R. Ambedkar and Jyoti Bai Phule.

Note: K.S. Saxena; "**Political History of Kashmir**" = the study of Mehabooba Mufti's cabinet = downfall of the Brahmin historians like Satish Chandra (JNU), Irfan Habib (Aligarh Muslim University) = Rakeshes Vidya ka dor, pp. 1-16.

Index